children who are sometimes contemporaneous with the younger man and decide whether to have children of their own?

Bringing individuality and spirit to an exploration of the changing roles of men and women, many older woman/younger man couples are building lasting, fulfilling, remarkably conflict-free relationships. *The Age Taboo* casts light not only on how the older woman/younger man relationship can work, but on the fundamental nature of any successful emotional commitment between two people.

Arlene Derenski and Sally B. Landsburg are licensed marriage and family therapists in private practice. With three other associates, they constitute Main Street Counseling Associates in Venice, California.

THE AGE TABOO

THE AGE TABOO

Older Women—Younger Men
Relationships

Arlene Derenski
Sally B. Landsburg

Little, Brown and Company   Boston-Toronto

FIRST EDITION

The authors are grateful to *CoEvolution Quarterly* for permission to quote from "Cross Generation Marriage" by Theodora Kroeber Quinn (Fall, 1976); *Human Behavior* for permission to quote from "Who's Afraid of Phyllis Chesler?" by Janet Chase-Marshall (September, 1979); *Newsweek* for permission to quote from "How Men Are Changing" (January 16, 1978); and the Los Angeles Times Syndicate for permission to quote from "An Indian Summer of the Heart" by Roderick Mann (May 23, 1978). Copyright © 1978 by the Los Angeles Times Syndicate.

Library of Congress Cataloging in Publication Data

Derenski, Arlene.
  The age taboo.

  Bibliography: p.
  Includes index.
  1. Interpersonal relations. 2. Commitment (Psychology). 3. Unmarried couples. 4. Middle-aged women. 5. Young men. 6. Marriage. I. Landsburg, Sally B. II. Title. III. Title: Older women— Younger men relationships.
  HM132.D469   306.7   81-1747
  ISBN 0-316-51366-0   AACR2

MV

Designed by Rosalie H. Davis

Published simultaneously in Canada by Little, Brown & Company (Canada) Limited

PRINTED IN THE UNITED STATES OF AMERICA

For Andy Reichline and Dan Derenski,
with whom we live out the ideas expressed on these pages.

ACKNOWLEDGMENTS

To begin with, we want to acknowledge all of the couples and individuals who allowed us access to the intimate details of their lives and feelings. Without these interviews there would be no book.

Second, our profoundest thanks to our business partner, Linda Buzzell-Saltzman, for her friendship, her support, and for assisting us with her expertise as a writer. Also, we thank our associate, Larry Buzzell-Saltzman, for holding down our therapy group while we went off to write.

In addition, we would like to thank the following people for their interest and their enthusiastic support: Natalie Lessinger, Jack Lessinger, Shelley List, Win Griffen, Arlene Spivak, Phyllis Bagdadi, Barbara Biggs, Francine Baker, Chris Conrad, Samuel Mor, Stephen Collins, and Betsy and Ron Isroelit.

Furthermore, we are grateful to our graduate school, the California Family Study Center in Burbank, California, for our training in relationship counseling and family therapy. In particular we would like to thank Dr. Clinton E. Phillips for developing such a rich graduate program.

Our most sincere appreciation to our editor, Genevieve Young, for her endless encouragement and her determination to help us create a book of which we could all be proud.

We very specially thank our typist, Joanne Barnett, first of all for working her way through our transcripts as well as our scribbly handwriting, and then for laboring over all these revisions. And Ginger Cowan, for helping us finish up the typing of odds and ends.

And, last but not least, our loving thanks to Andy Reichline and Dan Derenski, for patiently and continuously reading and rereading the pages of this manuscript as well as listening, suggesting, editing, and comforting whenever those services were needed.

CONTENTS

THE AGE TABOO

1 ⋆

A CONTROVERSIAL RELATIONSHIP

WHEN IT BECAME APPARENT THAT FORTY-ONE-YEAR-old Susan Howard and Peter Levin, twenty-six, were romantically involved, Susan's family and friends were surprised but shrugged philosophically. After all, the affair couldn't possibly last long. Everyone assumed that Susan was having a fling to soothe her wounded pride. Her husband of nineteen years had recently left her to marry another woman. They all agreed that Peter was a nice boy, just what Susan needed to help restore her confidence. Peter's friends saw the relationship as harmless, another extension of his education.

Then Peter moved into Susan's luxurious home, and reaction sharpened. "Susan, do you really know what you're doing? He's just a kid. How in the world can he possibly support you? You don't really intend to stay with him?"

Peter's friends from the radical sixties implied that he had sold out to the establishment. His parents were worried. They had expected him to settle down in the near future with a girl his own age. "Peter, don't you want a family of your own? Susan is a lovely woman, but she's so much older than you.

How are you going to feel about her ten or fifteen years from now?"

Six years later Susan and Peter are still living together. They are planning to be married soon and their families and friends have finally decided that the relationship works. Over the years, distrust has subsided into acceptance, but Susan recalls, "I was amazed by the extent of everyone's disapproval once they realized our intentions were honorable."

When an older woman and a younger man openly contemplate a permanent relationship, unsolicited advice flows thick and fast. Although concern comes largely from families, friends, and associates, even people who barely know the couple feel impelled to give warning of potential dangers. And along with those dire predictions, endless questions hurtle through their respective social strata.

What kind of man would marry an older woman? Is he looking for a mother? Or is he just interested in her body, her money, or her ability to help him get ahead? Can he accept that she may be more professionally successful than he? Will she have more influence than he in the relationship? Is the younger man aware of how seriously this choice can affect his life?

And what does the older woman see in him? Some people are sure that she is looking for the fulfillment of a sexual fantasy. But she'll regret it when she is withered and he is still at the peak of his form. Others believe that she wants a man she can dominate. It can't work anyway. He's much too immature. She'll get over it and then she'll want a real man. A lifelong marriage between an older woman and a younger man is impossible.

What is there about the older woman/younger man relationship that evokes such anxious questioning, so many derisive opinions, such intensity of feeling? Are the questions, opinions, and predictions that people offer about such a relationship merely reflections of their own ingrained beliefs about how men and women are supposed to behave? Or are the assumptions true? Whether there is any reality to these ideas is a matter that seriously concerns us, the authors, because we are both involved in committed relationships with men who are considerably younger than we are.

Our investigation into the phenomenon of older woman/ younger man relationships began with this fact. In addition, we are family therapists in private clinical practice. As professionals, we focus our expertise on helping troubled relationships. Whatever we could discover about the nature of older woman/younger man relationships — whether the couples had insurmountable problems, whether they were happier or unhappier, or whether they were more similar to than different from other marriages — was bound to be helpful to us.

To this end, we conducted tape-recorded interviews with fifty couples in committed relationships, either marriages or long-term living-together arrangements. Each interview lasted two to three hours. We interviewed six couples in greater depth, separately and together and over a period of time. In addition, we also did twelve interviews with individuals who had had at one time significant relationships with an older woman or a younger man. We chose to focus on couples who were already committed to each other. And we decided to change the names and occupations of the people we interviewed, in order to protect their privacy.

Other books, as well as plays and films, have been written about this subject, but most of them treat the older woman/ younger man couple as a brief encounter. The emphasis is on a temporary, primarily sexual, relationship. We wanted to know what happens when an older woman and a younger man decide to make their relationship permanent.

To get subjects, we simply told everyone we knew that we were looking for older woman/younger man couples. Offers for interviews poured in. We were surprised at the ease with which we found subjects, and long after the interviews were finished the calls kept coming. By the time we had done half of the interviews, we noticed repeating patterns in the information. We stopped at fifty couples when it became apparent that we were getting the same responses from all our interviewees.

Before picking the couples to interview, we had to decide in which of the relationships we were offered did the woman qualify as an "older woman." Since no one can say with authority just how much older is "older," we arbitrarily decided the age difference was to be six or more years, a significant enough difference to cause social problems. We did find two couples with an age difference of more than fifty years, although this extreme age gap is rare. Four couples were twenty to twenty-six years apart. All the rest ranged from six to eighteen years apart. The women were from twenty-seven to seventy-eight years old. The men's ages ranged from seventeen to fifty-one. In most cases the man was in his twenties or thirties while the woman was in her thirties, forties, or fifties.

At the time of the interviews the average duration of the relationships we observed was from one to ten years, but we also interviewed a few couples who had been married for twenty to thirty years. Nearly all of the women, and about half the men, have been married before. Three-fourths of the women have children from an earlier marriage, most of whom are at least teenaged or in their early twenties. Only five men had children from a previous marriage, and these children were almost all under twelve. Two older women/younger men couples had a child together. Two other couples were planning to have a child.

Most of the people we interviewed now live on the West Coast, but many of them originally came from other places in the United States or other parts of the world. We also talked to couples who live in the eastern and southeastern parts of the United States. In addition, we interviewed individuals and couples in England, France, Italy, Spain, and Israel. Allowing for the differences in personal background and culture, the comments of most of these couples were remarkably similar.

As we progressed through our interviews, each new couple eagerly questioned us about our own relationships with our younger spouses as well as about other older woman/younger man couples. They suspected that other such couples were experiencing the same joys and frustrations that they were, but they rarely had the opportunity to find out. They were eager to hear what we had found out about the problems of an older woman/younger man relationship and they were even more interested in the suggestions or solutions we offered concerning the future.

People who were not involved in an older woman/younger man relationship were almost as interested. Women, in general, are very curious about it. They usually start their questioning with something like "Can this relationship possibly last?" and then go on to "What do I do about telling him how old I am? What do I talk to him about? Can I call him up? How do I meet a younger man? In a singles bar, a disco? What are people going to think? What's he going to think of me? Is my fragile ego going to be crushed? What happens when the sexual attraction wears off? Am I going to get hurt or abandoned? Is it really going to be fun and exciting? Will I feel wicked and sexy? In the long run, what's going to happen to us?"

A woman's list of questions reads like a catalogue of her primary life concerns: security and respectability. She worries about aging, about desirability, about self-esteem, and circles

back again to security. She is intrigued, but she is also afraid.
Women are curious but hesitant about relationships with
younger men. The feasibility of such a relationship on a long-
term basis is a recurring issue for many of the unmarried female clients we see in private practice. Women clients tell us
they have been in worthwhile relationships with younger men,
but left the men because of feeling guilty about the associa-
tion and anxious about the future.

Women's feelings about relationships with younger men,
and their questions about those feelings, suggest a need to
explore the origin of their fears. They also need, if they are
going to consider such relationships for themselves, some
legitimate knowledge about how relationships between older
women and younger men really work.

And what are the alternatives for women over thirty-five? A
mature woman might be interested in the potential of an
older woman/younger man relationship because of the limited selection of acceptable same-age partners. In our experience, the older and more accomplished a woman is, the
narrower her choices are. A successful writer told us, "A lot
of the time I feel men my own age are threatened by me or
want to control me. I'm tired of making men uncomfortable
or dodging their attempts to manipulate me."

The choices are even further decreased by the fact that
older men frequently prefer younger women. Our society
tends to discard women over thirty-five.

An attractive forty-three-year-old widow complained, "I
would be ready to marry again, but most of the men I meet
who are my age, men who are warm, interested, and interesting, are happily married and have every intention of staying
that way. This really reduces my options for finding a new
relationship."

Relationships between older women and younger men can

increase the possible choices of partners for mature women. According to Norman Rockmael, leader of singles' events in Los Angeles, "It's the women over forty, who are aware, intelligent, attractive and assertive, who have the most difficulty being single. They pose a threat to men. They either have to give themselves permission to date younger men, which is still tough to do today, or give up some assertiveness and merge their identity with the man's. If she doesn't do this, she has to give up a life with men. Neither's a bargain."[1]

Most of the women we interviewed have made major life changes. Nearly all of them have been married, divorced, reared children, largely by themselves, and have learned to be self-sufficient. Many have responded powerfully to the women's movement. They expect to live their lives as effective, productive individuals. They are unwilling to live simply for the sake of having a partner with men who do not meet their needs. But only recently has our social environment loosened up enough to allow people to consider openly the possibilities of such a pairing.

A forty-seven-year-old New York executive involved with a man eleven years her junior commented, "The change in the social climate has a lot to do with this phenomenon. I know I wouldn't have been able to have a relationship with a younger man fifteen years ago, or maybe even ten years ago."

Men are also affected by the changes that are occurring in our society. According to an article in a 1978 edition of *Newsweek* entitled, "How Men Are Changing," younger men are most at ease with the new openness. They are less obsessed, on the whole, with seeming masculine, and they are more willing to accept as given what their fathers would not have dreamed of — the equal importance of their female partners' life goals.[2]

Yet the questions that men under the age of thirty-five

ask about older woman/younger man relationships are very different from those asked by women. Several men whom we queried were concerned about how it would feel when the woman crossed the border into really old age or about the fact that she might be likely to die sooner than he. A man wonders if there would be a really big gap in experience level. "Would my values be different from hers as a result of generational differences?" he asks. "If she has more money, would there be problems between us in terms of issues like money and power? Would I have to adapt myself to her way of life rather than having her adapt to mine? Would I have to miss or simply say good-bye to certain stages of my life in order to catch up or stay in tune with her? But maybe it would be fun just to sit back and let myself be taken care of. It might be nice not to have to pay anyone else's bills. Still, what if she has more say in the relationship than I do?"

Just as the women's questions reflect their anxieties, men's questions mirror their own concerns. Issues of prestige, power, and dominance pervade the men's queries. He wonders how he will be regarded if his woman is not young and pretty. He worries that greater experience or more money may mean that her life takes precedence over his. And shouldn't the woman be following in the man's lead and not vice versa?

The questions that men and women ask about what will happen to them if they attempt an older woman/younger man relationship describe the issues that most deeply affect their respective sexes: women's questions relate to security; men's questions refer to power. They indicate that the conventional male and female roles may be jeopardized or, worse still, reversed. An entire belief system about the ways in which men and women are supposed to behave in marriages is threatened by the older woman/younger man couple.

Yet people continue to be extraordinarily interested in finding out about older woman/younger man relationships. They become even more interested when informed that the relationship is not just a passing affair. "How can people risk such an unconventional relationship," we are asked, "when the acceptable marriages around us are falling apart left and right?"

One of the possibilities is that people who are involving themselves in older woman/younger man relationships may be seeking a viable alternative to a style of marriage that no longer fits them. Maybe there is something special going on in the older woman/younger man relationship that most people don't know about. Perhaps there are aspects of these relationships that make men and women who have been influenced by the extraordinary changes in our society over the past fifty years prefer them.

What are younger men and older women looking for when they form relationships with each other? We would like to suggest the possibility that these pairings might hold some fresh solutions to the age-old problem of how two human beings, with distinctly different social and sexual conditioning, are supposed to live together. Perhaps these couples have learned something about themselves, each other, and relationships that might serve as a model for improving the quality of marriages in general.

This brings us to our bias. We believe that marriage between an older woman and a younger man is an acceptable choice. It may even be a desirable choice for certain kinds of men and women in today's world. This belief has naturally influenced the shape and direction of this book. Because we are both personally and professionally dedicated to the creation of successful relationships, we have focused on the workings of healthy, long-term relationships. In examining relationships that work well, we may have opportunities to learn what creates success, and how that knowledge may be applied.

In our investigation of the phenomenon we have tried to capture the essence of older women/younger men couples through their words and through our observations. We have attempted to draw a picture of older women with younger men in our time, a time of immense and rapid social change. While we did interview several older woman/younger man couples who lived in traditional ways, most of these couples were developing a new type of relationship, which may become one of the dominant styles of the future. We will examine the ways our interviewees have found to cope with the changing roles of women and men. We take a look at how the age difference assists or hinders their adaptation and discuss the problems they face.

Controversial ideas and values wind through this book and spill from the mouths of our interviewees. Some of our conclusions contradict popularly held beliefs about how older women/younger men relationships operate.

Basically, older women and younger men are like all other people. They work, they have families, they have friends, they have the problems that any other couple has. For our investigation we asked them to focus on their age difference, something most of them do only occasionally in their lives. Many couples have told us that they rarely notice that the woman is older than the man, so it is fair to say our interviewees are more like other people than they are different from them.

In today's society we think of marriages as occurring between people who are the same age. Relationships in which the man is older than the woman are also acceptable. Logically, there is a third alternative, a partnering in which the woman is older than the man. But when men or women make this choice, the response is generally negative. Accepted cultural patterns die hard.

On that subject Margaret Mead once said, ". . . If we had a

notion of every possible combination — man older, woman older . . . then no one pattern would be regarded as peculiar. We would remark on them in the way we say: 'These people go to Europe every year, and those people never go to the country in the summer.' They would just be interesting differences."[3] Perhaps our book will encourage a greater acceptance of this point of view.

2 ·

WHO ARE THEY?

WHAT KIND OF PERSON GETS INVOLVED IN AN OLDER woman/younger man relationship? Has the older woman/younger man relationship always existed, or is it a phenomenon of the permissive nineteen-seventies? Do people who commit themselves to such a relationship have a particular sort of personality, or share a similar attitude? Before we embarked on our interviews, we decided to see whether answers to any of these questions had already been discovered, so we looked into what had previously been written on the subject.

Library research into the topic of older women with younger men produced little pertinent material. Although we cross-referenced the idea in every way imaginable, no psychological or sociological studies turned up on long-term relationships in which the woman is older than the man. The very lack of investigative material about these relationships reconfirmed our belief that the subject needed to be explored.

Historical accounts of older women/younger men relationships consist largely of writings about celebrities of their own times. The Prophet Muhammad, Napoleon Bonaparte, William Shakespeare, Benjamin Disraeli, and Robert Louis Stevenson were all considerably younger than their wives. Nineteenth-century novelist George Sand had long-lasting liaisons with two younger men, Frédéric Chopin and Alexandre Manceau. Lady Randolph Churchill was married to two men who were very much younger than she, and Elizabeth Barrett was older than her husband, Robert Browning.

Biographical reference to these older woman/younger man relationships exists only because these people were famous enough to have the details of their lives recorded. Documentation from earlier times also tells us that older women/younger men relationships were not common, but that they did occur and often lasted for the duration of the couple's lifetime. There is no way of knowing exactly what the future will bring — whether there will be more or fewer older women/younger men relationships. However, in terms of the public attention that these relationships have recently received, there is some indication that the partnering of women with younger men may be on the increase.

Over the last few years articles on the subject have appeared in *Ms.* magazine, *Newsweek*, *Time*, *Cosmopolitan*, *Playgirl*, *US*, and *Ebony*. The approaches and tones of the articles vary. The treatment has ranged from interviews and social commentary to gossip and psychiatric platitudes. But whatever the point of view of the article, one fact is clear: older women/younger men relationships are news.

What we had originally perceived as a series of personal experiences on the part of a few people is turning into something of a social phenomenon. Certainly, so far as celebrities go, older women/younger men relationships are not limited to a few isolated instances.

A host of people in the public eye have been interviewed, written about, and gossiped about since the subject of older women with younger male partners has become newsworthy.

Suddenly we are told that Ruth Gordon, star of *Harold and Maude*, who has been quietly married to author-director Garson Kanin for thirty-six years, is sixteen years older than her husband. Mystery writer Agatha Christie was married for forty-five years to the archeologist Max Mallowan, who was fourteen years her junior. Nora Kaye, the former prima ballerina who is now a film producer, has been married to director Herb Ross (*The Turning Point, The Goodbye Girl*), ten years her junior, for seventeen years. And actress Louise Fletcher, forty-seven, lived with Morgan Mason, twenty-three, for several years.

And the list goes on. Kate Jackson, of television's "Charlie's Angels," is married to actor Andrew Stevens, who is seven years younger than Ms. Jackson. Sybil Burton Christopher is fifty. Her husband, Jordan Christopher, is thirty-eight. Everyone said the match wouldn't last. That was fourteen years ago. Dinah Shore is eighteen years older than Burt Reynolds, with whom she had a four-year love affair.

Singer Grace Slick has twice married a man who was younger than she. Actress Estelle Parsons has been living for several years with New York University law professor Peter Zimroth, who is fourteen years younger than Miss Parsons. The African singer Miriam Makeba is ten years older than her husband, Stokely Carmichael. Robert Wolders, married to the late Merle Oberon, was twenty years younger than his wife. Lucille Ball has been married to Gary Morton, twelve years younger, for almost twenty years.

Public figures in older women/younger men relationships are not necessarily limited to the entertainment world. Former Congresswoman Yvonne Braithwaite Burke is five years older than her husband, William Burke. Mystery writer Raymond Chandler, creator of the detective hero, Philip Marlowe, was married for thirty years to a woman who was almost eighteen years older than he. Taylor Caldwell, seventy-eight, historical novelist and grande dame of the American historical novel, is married to William Robert Prestie, sixty-one. Writer Dorothy Parker was in a twenty-year, off-again, on-again marriage with Alan Campbell, eleven years her junior.

In Erica Jong's latest novel, *How to Save Your Own Life*, the heroine, a well-known novelist and poet who is a thinly veiled autobiographical figure, visits Hollywood and falls in love with a younger man. The young man is a writer himself and the son of another famous writer. The last half of the novel revolves around the heroine's decision to risk going on with the relationship in the face of her own fears about the future. In real life Erica Jong, now thirty-seven, lived for several years with Jonathan Fast, six years younger, the son of Howard Fast. Recently they were married and have produced a daughter, Molly Miranda Jong-Fast.

These are people who are seriously involved with each other. Their relationships are not fleeting affairs. Whether married, living together, or simply in an exclusive relationship, each couple has remained as a couple for a considerable period of time. Most contemporary relationships do not endure longer than theirs.

And they are only a handful out of many. A recent newspaper article about the United States stated that in approximately 4 percent of the married population, wives are older than their husbands. We are inclined to think this figure is conservative. Since a wife's being older than her husband is still not a completely acceptable notion, a woman whose husband is younger tends to fudge a bit about her age. In addition, the figure does not take into account people who are living together without being married.

Yet history, contemporary gossip, and statistics give us only a fragmentary picture. Let us see what more we can learn from direct encounters with people actually living within such an arrangement. We have picked three couples whose

stories we would like to share. They come from varied backgrounds and each couple's choice of marriage styles is different from those of the other two. In addition, we have
deliberately chosen couples with increasing age differences
between the man and the woman, to see if the relationship
is more stressful as the age difference gets larger.

Jeff Courtney-Fein and Barbara Courtney-Fein are married
but retain their respective names and identities. Their wedding announcement sports a photograph of them seated in a
lacy wrought iron love seat on the front porch of a white clap-
board house, looking every inch the southern gentleman and
his demure bride. Engraved over the photograph is the word
"Finally . . ." Inside, the announcement says, "We made it
legal! On May 6, 1978, we became Mr. and Ms. Jeff Courtney
and Barbara Fein." Before that date Jeff and Barbara had
been living together for five years.

Jeff is thirty, Barbara is thirty-eight. Barbara has never been
married before; Jeff was married briefly many years ago.
Neither of them has children. Barbara started her professional
life as an actress and then developed into a writer. Her first
book has done extremely well and she has just signed a contract for a second. Jeff is a photographer, cinematographer,
and author of a book that is a photographic documentation
of life in the bayou country where he grew up. The book has
been very well received, particularly in Cajun country. As Jeff
says, "They may not know me in Los Angeles, but back where
I come from, I'm a star."

Barbara grins her delight. They are obviously pleased with
each other and their respective accomplishments. They are
both intense personalities, but Barbara fires off her comments
in machine-gun bursts, while Jeff is more deliberate. Barbara
started to tell us how they met and at what point they discovered each other's ages.

"The house I had been living in with a roommate had burned down and I was temporarily living by myself in the home of a friend who was out of town. Jeff called my roommate, who was an old friend of his and asked, 'Can you put me up for a few days?' and she said, 'Well, there's not enough room where I'm staying, but Barbara is living in this huge place. Maybe she can help you.' So he calls me."

At this point Jeff broke in. "I was waiting to hear about a grant and I stayed there about eight or ten days."

Barbara continued, "Actually, I didn't really want him in that house at all. It wasn't personal; I didn't know him. My mother had just died and I really wanted to be alone. However, here was this young starving artist and I just didn't feel like I could say no. So I said, 'Well, if you want to sleep on the couch, fine; if you want to bring a sleeping bag, fine; just stay out of my hair.' But he flirted around and he came on, and by the third night I just couldn't resist him."

Barbara stopped and thought a minute. "I don't know how the subject of age came up. God knows we had talked about everything else at that point. I know I thought he was older and he thought I was younger. At some point I said, 'Well, how old are you anyway?' And he said, 'Twenty-four.' This was six years ago. At that time I was thirty-two years old. It sounded like he was such a baby. I just got kind of hysterical and he said, 'Why? How old are you?' I said, 'I'm thirty-two.' He said, 'Aw, come on,' and I said, 'Yeah, thirty-two.'"

Jeff said reflectively, "I guess I was surprised by the age difference, but outside of that it didn't mean much to me."

We asked Barbara Courtney-Fein what it was that specifically appealed to her about Jeff.

"I know that I felt differently about Jeff. It was not an infatuation for me. I really thought this guy could be a good partner for me. And I'd never really thought about a man in those terms before. But with Jeff I really felt that he'd be the right person for me. A companion and a friend, as well as a lover."

Barbara once told Jeff that he was the best girlfriend she had. When we checked with Barbara about the implication of that comment, she said, "What I meant is that I feel the same degree of intimacy, trust, and supportiveness with Jeff as I would feel with a close woman friend."

Barbara described to us what she wanted in a man and how her ideas fit Jeff. "My ideal of a human being is connected to my belief in the principle of the Yin and the Yang. I think we all have complementary masculine and feminine characteristics. I do not care for macho men, and I've never liked ultrafeminine, drippy women. I like very balanced beings, and Jeff's very balanced. He's capable of what I would consider a lot of feminine traits such as tenderness, understanding, and interest in details of life as well as the more masculine things of being very aggressive, steady, and strong. He has three overall characteristics that are important to me: steadfastness, his ability to express his femininity, and his wonderful, zany sense of humor."

Barbara herself is a determined, decisive person. She lives intensely, not wasting a moment. Jeff Courtney-Fein likes that. We wanted to know what else he likes about Barbara, what would draw him into commitment to a woman eight years older than he.

Jeff said, "To begin with, she's got a terrific sense of humor. And Barbara is a professional woman, which is important to me. She has her own career and devotes a lot of energy to it; she has some very impressive accomplishments. But she also cares a lot about me. She takes an enormous interest in what I'm doing, and that means a lot to me. We're very good friends as well as lovers and it's a friendship that I've become rather dependent upon. It's something I like. I've gotten to where I hate to go away a long time without her. We're very close to each other; we spend a lot of time with each other. I'm not the most tolerant person around and I get bored easily with people. I appreciate our relationship, particularly our friendship."

At this point in their relationship, following their individual careers still separates them, often for months at a time. When they are separated, they miss each other terribly, but both Jeff and Barbara continue to function well by themselves. The qualities they value in each other are similar: independence, androgyny — a combination of masculine and feminine traits — ambition, career orientation and development of one's own creative potential. And most important in the older woman/ younger man relationship, friendship! A genuine caring about what the other person is, does, and thinks.

Barbara and Jeff are one kind of older woman/younger man relationship. Their life-style as a married couple is rather unconventional. Their insistence on maintaining separate identities, including separate names, is not necessarily typical of the older woman/younger man relationship. Many people who are in this kind of relationship have quite conventional marriage styles.

Mary and Mike Bayer are one such couple. They met when Mary was thirty-nine and Mike was twenty-four. They were married six months later. The Bayers live in a well-to-do suburban town just outside Los Angeles. They have been married for three years. Mike grew up in the same town where they live now. Mary was raised in the Midwest. This is Mike's first marriage. Mary was married at eighteen, and at the time they met, her three sons were fifteen, eighteen, and twenty. She had been divorced for about three years before she met Mike. Both Mary and Mike are outgoing people. They are both extremely direct about who they are and what they want.

It's hard to tell that there is a significant age difference between Mary and Mike. We first met them when Mary was about seven months pregnant with their son. Mike has the deportment of a much older person, while Mary seems astonishingly young. Mary walked in the door, positively glowing, looking about twenty-five years old. She has brown hair, bright blue eyes, and a dewy tan that any teenager would envy. We don't know exactly what we expected to see, but we were somewhat taken aback that this woman simply showed no signs of aging at all.

We were to experience this sense of surprise again and again; it is difficult to pinpoint the age of most of the women we've interviewed. Even when we know approximately how old she must be from the ages of her children, when she tells us her actual age it's always a shock. Generally, she appears to be younger. On the other hand, a number of the men have a level of behavioral maturity that partially closes the age gap. As a result, the actual age difference is often greater than one would assume at first glance.

Mary settled herself in a comfortable spot on the floor, stuffed some cushions behind her back, tossed her hair out of her eyes, and started telling us about her life.

"I was born and raised on a farm in Iowa and I'm the oldest of six children. I moved to California with my first husband when my oldest son was three months old. Most of my adult life I've been a housewife, but about eight years ago some things changed for me. I guess I just had to prove something to myself. For a long time my ex-husband had me believing that I wasn't intelligent enough to get a decent job. I had to prove to him that I was, so I went back to school and got two years of college in and got this job being head of the Junior High Library. Well, I proved that I could do it. But it's really not all that great, working and raising a family, so after the baby is born I just want to sit back for a little bit."

Mary Bayer has no particular urge to set the world on fire,

but she did need to prove to herself that she could go to college, get a job, and perform competently. Although she is basically happy being a homemaker right now, she has no intention of ever giving up her desire for learning. However, working outside her home is something she will save for a later period in her life, when her new son is older.

Mike is more than willing for Mary to stay home and take care of the family. He works with his father as an orthopedist. They manufacture braces and artificial limbs. Mike makes hospital calls and fits people for braces. As an orthopedist, Mike is no stranger to the tragedy of other people. How does he feel about his own life while working in a world so filled with pain?

"Maybe all those misanthropic people who think the world is going to crap are right, but I am going to be happy. I am going to build something and enjoy it and have fun in my life."

Mike Bayer comes from a very different background from Mary's. He grew up in southern California, the youngest son of comfortably-off parents. His two older brothers graduated from high school and went to college. One is a doctor and the other is a dentist. Mike was the rebel.

Mike loves his family and they love him, but he has to do things his own way. One of those things is taking on a thirty-nine-year-old wife and three stepsons, including one stepson who is only three years younger than he.

Mike and Mary first got acquainted at the home of a mutual friend. Neither of them was really aware of the extent of the age difference until the second or third time they met. By that time they had both communicated their interest in each other to their mutual friend, and shortly after that they started dating. Since Mike looks much older than he actually is, and Mary looks younger, any physical discrepancy in their appearance together is almost negligible.

Mary told us that what had attracted her to Mike was that he was someone she could talk to. We asked her if she could explain a little bit more.

"After my divorce, when I started dating, I always found myself being bored and I didn't know why. At first it would seem there were a lot of things in common but after a short period of time I found I really didn't have anything to say to that person anymore. It used to bother me. I thought because I hadn't finished college that I just wasn't educated enough and assumed I was boring to them too. Then I met Mike and he hadn't had any more education than I had, and yet it seems like we can always find things to talk about. He loves to read. A lot of times we'll read together. I give myself credit for not wanting to stay the same, for wanting to change, like I'll probably always want to go to school, better myself, change myself. Mike is the same way. He's so eager to learn new things all the time; he's always reading, he just keeps life interesting."

We asked Mike Bayer what he likes about his wife.

"Mary has such an orderly life. She manages her time and doesn't let loose ends build around her. She does the things that have to be done first and then relaxes and enjoys herself. I like her stable nature. I also like her three boys, and they are part of her. Being with the boys gave me a chance to gain some self-respect and let me assume a responsible role. I like challenges, and helping Mary out with her kids made me feel really good. And there's another thing. I've always associated with people that I have something to learn from, and I feel that I can learn a lot from Mary. Actually, we both learn a lot from each other."

Mike and Mary Bayer share a love of family, home, and children, a desire to be productive people who have a positive attitude toward life and a love of learning. The way they choose to live their lives is quite different from the way the Courtney-Feins have decided to live theirs.

The Trentons live yet another way. Barry is twenty-eight and Jenna, fifty-four. Barry Trenton is a soft-spoken, six-foot-four-inch teddy bear. His height is softened by longish hair, a big curving mustache and the fifty extra pounds he carries. He smokes elaborate pipes and speaks with a British accent. He has been in the United States for four years. He recalls a conventional middle-class English childhood. After high school he worked for two years and, at nineteen, began college. He studied education and became a teacher. After college, Barry joined the Voluntary Service Overseas, the British equivalent of the Peace Corps. For two years he taught high school in Jamaica and then came to the United States.

Jenna is an electronics engineer, widely recognized for outstanding contributions to her own profession. Barry is her fifth husband. She has been divorced three times, widowed once, and has two grown sons.

She is matronly and makes no effort to disguise the fact. She is simply not concerned about her physical appearance. Her interests lie in other areas: her work, her hobbies, and her friends, who feel that Jenna should be enshrined as a national treasure. She tells elaborate, hilarious stories spiced with witty bits of ironic understatement. She has extensive knowledge in many fields, which she imparts laced with her dry and delicious humor. She is, without question, an extraordinary person.

Barry and Jenna met at the company where they both worked. Barry had been hired to repair equipment, and they became friends with neither one seeing the other as a potential partner. Barry had relationships with other women at the time, but he and Jenna became buddies. They kept each other company, went drinking together, and worked on Jenna's project of the moment, a boat that she was building in her backyard. Much of Jenna's social life revolved around the Folklore Society, in which she was an ardent participator. Barry was soon accepted into the group and felt at home with them.

The age difference was never an issue with them. They knew each other's relative ages from the beginning of the acquaintance. Since they had not planned on falling in love, it never occurred to them to think much about it. As their feelings for each other deepened, the transition from intimate friends to lovers seemed the most natural thing in the world. It took about six months for their relationship to grow from a friendship into a love affair. After another six months Barry and Jenna were married.

We asked Barry to tell us what attracted him to a woman twenty-six years older than he.

"She is the most incredible person I've ever met in my life. A real woman. She appreciates my singing and guitar playing, which very few people do. She is absolutely delighted when I do the washing up — which I think is my duty. She is just an incredible woman. She comes up with things that are absolutely fantastic and creative. She's an artist; she paints. She's also one of the world's top engineers. And she is interested in me, which is very good for my ego."

When we first called Jenna to ask for an interview she told us that she had been married several times but that this was the best marriage. In our interview we asked her to explain why.

"Barry's the nicest man I've ever met and also the nicest fellow I've ever married. Finally, after all this time I am able to relate to a guy who wants to take care of me and do all the wonderful things that I always thought I wanted but mostly couldn't stand."

We wanted to know more about what Jenna meant.

"He's a nurturing man. Oh, he calls me about six times a day just to say hello while I'm at work. He does all of those little things like getting up and getting me a drink of water in the middle of the night. I take care of him, too, but he returns it. I'm not used to men who return it to this extent. And if he knows I don't want to do something he generally does it. You know, women think they want this kind of man but if they get one they can't bear it. Had I known him when I was twenty it probably wouldn't have worked at all. I would have felt hemmed in, held down, overrun; I wouldn't have been willing to accept this interdependency."

Barry Trenton told us that he enjoys the warmth and security of family life, but without the rigid sameness of his childhood. With Jenna he has found the opportunity to combine the various influences of his life. He and Jenna share an independent spirit, a strong ethical code, and a well-developed sense of humor.

The experiences of the Courtney-Feins, the Bayers, and the Trentons provide some answers to the questions people often ask about the older woman/younger man relationship. While the answers are by no means definitive, they do point away from the usual preconceptions. Let us look at some of these questions.

One of the questions we are most often asked is "Where do you go to meet a younger man?" as if there were some separate, distinct place where hordes of younger men are just sitting around, waiting to be picked like apples. Since many people assume that the only function of an older woman/younger man relationship is sexual, their idea of where to meet a younger man might be a bar or a disco: in other words, a place to pick someone up.

The people we interviewed met each other in the same situations where they might meet a man or a woman their own age. The Courtney-Feins met through a friend, the Bayers did likewise, and the Trentons met at work. Other people met in similar situations — mutual friends, parties, work, clubs, church activities, or college classes. Two couples whom we talked to were introduced by the woman's children, who had taken a fancy to the younger man. Mutual liking turned into friendship and from there into consideration of a long-term relationship.

What we learned was that where an older woman or a younger man meet is not important, but the attitude with which they approach each other is very significant. The men and women we have talked to have not set age limits on friendships or other potential relationships.

Had the people we interviewed dated older women or younger men before? Some had, some had not.

Until he met Jenna, Barry Trenton had not had any relationships with women who were older than he. Mike Bayer's experience was quite different. He has always dated women who were older than he. Mike told us: "When I was sixteen I was dating women nineteen to twenty-two, and when I was twenty-three or twenty-four, I would date a woman in her mid-thirties. I dated women who were attractive to me; I don't consider age a barrier."

We asked Mike if he had ever wondered about why he picked older women. He said, "I consider myself of above average intelligence; generally above the norm of women my own age. I find older women more intelligent than teenagers or women in their early twenties. The younger ones don't have the culture, the style, the charm; they just don't have it."

Jeff Courtney talked about his attitude toward women who are older than he. "When I was twenty-four, I was drawn to a lot of older women, that is, women over twenty-four. I guess I feel older women are just more interesting. There is a lot more to discuss; their experiences are broader. When Barbara and I met, we started out by having a lot of long talks because there was a variety of things and experiences to talk about."

Jeff Courtney and Mike Bayer's comments are reminiscent of the words of Theodora Kroeber-Quinn, a noted anthropologist who was married to a man almost fifty years younger than she. In an article on older women/younger men relationships published in *Co-Evolution Quarterly*, she characterized the men involved as being on an accelerated time track. To cross the generations in marriage, she says, a man must have "raced down his time track with greater awareness, speed and intensity than is customary."[1]

She described the men as persons who have always had a sense of being older than their chronological age, both intellectually and emotionally. We have often observed that when an older woman/younger man relationship is working out successfully, the man has an extraordinary level of personal development in many, but not necessarily all, aspects of his life.

For example, Alex is in his early thirties and has been dating older women since he was in his late teens. Alex grew up behind the Iron Curtain. He had worked, side by side, as a full partner with his father from the time he was a small boy. When he was twelve, his father was separated from the family for two years and sent to Siberia. During that time, Alex assumed full responsibility for his mother and baby brother. After his father returned, Alex continued to work with him. His parents have always treated Alex with the dignity and respect accorded another adult and expected him to produce on an adult level. There was no other choice. The family was in circumstances where Alex needed to pull his weight as a full-grown man long before it was time for him to become one.

Alex said to us, "The biggest reason I've mostly dated older women is that I am old. I never had a childhood to speak of. I have been thoroughly loved and generously indulged by both my parents, but due to our circumstances, there was just no time for me to be a kid. I simply have never had anything to say to women who are in their late teens or early twenties." A precocious maturity has made women his own age an inappropriate choice for Alex.

We wanted to know if Barbara Courtney-Fein had ever been disturbed by the idea of dating men who were younger than she. "No, I had dated younger men several times before and found it a very satisfactory arrangement," she said. "It never bothered me; in fact I think I was kind of tickled by it. I have come to the conclusion that certain kinds of women, like myself, who are independent and follow a career, are often far more compatible with younger men than older men. It's really hard for older men to allow women to have a career, to be independent, and to speak to waiters or what-have-you. That's always bothered me terribly because I'm not very good at playing those games. I can do it if I have to, but why put myself in that position? Younger guys are brought up in a different milieu and are more likely to let me be myself."

Jenna Trenton had occasionally dated men who were younger than she, but her previous marriages were to men in her age group or older than she. As a result, the idea of marrying Barry was startling to her. What convinced her that the marriage might work was their extraordinary compatibility. Mary Bayer told us much the same story. She had dated younger men, although never one as young as Mike. However, mutual regard grew so quickly that Mary soon relinquished her misgivings about the age difference.

When Agatha Christie, at the age of forty, met her husband-to-be, Max Mallowan, twenty-six, on a visit to an archeological dig in Iraq, she was impressed by the fact that a man so young should have so much knowledge and such grave maturity. They became friends and six months later Mallowan asked Mrs. Christie to marry him. Agatha Christie's response to her young suitor's proposal was typical. She was both surprised and confused.

"It had never occurred to me that Max and I would be or ever could be on those terms. We were friends. We had become instant and closer friends, it seemed to me, than I and any friend had ever been before. . . . I said immediately that I couldn't. He asked why couldn't I. I said for every reason. I was years older than he was — he admitted that, and said he had always wanted to marry someone older than he was. I said that was nonsense and it was a bad thing to do. . . . The only thing, I suppose, that I didn't say, and which naturally I would have said if I had felt it, was that I didn't want to marry him — because, quite suddenly, I felt that nothing in the world would be as delightful as being married to him. If only he was older or I was younger."[2]

Women who have considered committed relationships with younger men have repeatedly told us about the same unbidden thought that persisted in surfacing: "If he were only older or I were younger, it would be perfect."

What do they actually see in each other? What would a woman find in a man eight to fifteen years her junior? Why does a man choose to spend his life with a woman who may be many years older than he? The stories of our three couples seem to indicate that older women and younger men are attracted to each other for much the same sorts of reasons that any other couple is. Mutual interests, commonality of thought, genuine liking of the other person generally lead to warm feelings of friendship. As with any other couple, each often sees in the other what he or she most admires.

One last question about who chooses older women or younger men as mates remains to be explored. What type of person is likely to think seriously about a permanent commitment to an older woman/younger man relationship? Do these men and women have any personality characteristics in common? What influence might personality type have on the success of the relationship?

Let's examine a bit more of the background of the people involved in older woman/younger men relationships and see if any pattern of behavior and attitude emerges.

Barbara Courtney-Fein is a woman who had done everything her own way all of her life. Until she met Jeff, she was convinced she would never marry, figuring that most men could not adjust to her independence of thought and action, or to her ability to move in a direct line toward what she wants. Barbara told us the very first thing that appealed to her about Jeff was that he knew what he wanted.

"I was asking him about his plans and he said, 'Well, I looked around me and I thought, what am I doing with my life? I love photography and I can contribute to this trend of photographic books.' He's different. He figured everything out. He was logical in his thinking and then he carried through. He really did what he set out to do and his book got published. That kind of fortitude is very impressive to me."

Barbara and Jeff Courtney-Fein are both self-directed people. Each goes directly toward what he or she wants without being terribly concerned by what other people might think.

Mary Bayer's most vivid memory of her childhood is of having a great deal of responsibility. As the oldest child, she took care of younger brothers and sisters in addition to a wide range of house and farm chores. Looking back now, she feels that she had too much responsibility for a child, but that the experience was valuable for her in that it taught her to make independent decisions very early in her life. Mike was a city child, brought up in a well-to-do family who had high expectations for their children. Mike chose to do things differently. His brothers went to college, but Mike went out to live on his own to find out what the world was all about. He told us: "I felt like the black sheep of the family. I was in wild rebellion for a while. It's like something I read once: 'Two roads diverged in a wood, and I — I took the one less traveled by.'

As far as I am concerned, it has made all the difference. Now I have a fair idea of what I want. I wouldn't change a thing."

Since Mike had explained to us that he thought of himself as something of a rebel, we asked Mary how she saw both Mike and herself as individuals. Did she think of herself and Mike as unconventional people? Mary nodded slowly, then more emphatically.

"I would say that fits for both of us. I've always considered myself the rebel of the family; I'm not like anybody else in my family. I'm not the type that gets into a lot of trouble; I just don't think the same as they do. I have different kinds of ideas about what's important in life, about religion, about relationships with people. I think I'm different. I think Mike sees himself as being that way, too, not so much a rebel of the family anymore, but in life in general, he's a nonconformist and so am I."

Mike and Mary Bayer see themselves as noncomformists, but not radical. Our perception of most of the people we have interviewed is that they are rather unorthodox in their approach to life. None of them are persons who would go out of their way to flout social tradition, but neither are they overly concerned with appearances.

Jenna Trenton is a woman who has been liberated most of her life, far before the idea came into vogue. She grew up on a farm in a world of older adults. She was largely isolated from people her own age. Her grandparents and great-grandmother were self-sufficient people who had their own tough-minded ideas of how to live in the world. As a result, Jenna has lived life on her own terms, going her own way, at her own pace.

She explained to us: "I have never had any difficulty, for instance, in a job. I don't know that I've ever had a job where I was discriminated against because I was a woman. I've rarely run into that kind of prejudice. Once, I started working in an office and they told me that I couldn't smoke there. The men could but I couldn't. So I quit the job. Mostly, I don't know that I was ever in a situation where being female made a difference. When people are surprised by my position, then I'm surprised. Once a man came up to visit me and after three days he told me he had never known a woman in the position I was in. (Jenna was then the manager of the group.) It never occurred to me that I was in *any* position. After he left, I started to think about it."

Jenna has always taken for granted that she could do anything she wanted to do and she acted on that assumption.

Certain personality characteristics occur repeatedly in most of the people we interviewed. First, both the men and the women often perceive themselves as somehow different from other people and, to some extent, they see themselves as loners. They get along with other people, but are not crowd followers.

Second, they tend to be people who are not overly dependent on consistent social approval. They can be rather stubborn about self-determination even though their behavior may appear outwardly uncertain and sometimes erratic. Out of the fifty-odd couples we've interviewed, most of the people are used to taking responsibility for the fact that their life choices may be different from those of others. Psychologically speaking, we would characterize Barbara, Jeff, Mary, Mike, Barry, and Jenna as risk-taking personalities who can take the chance of doing something unusual without feeling crippling anxiety. Each one is relatively comfortable with being him- or herself. They believe they have chosen their mates well and are basically confident about the potential of their marriages.

Insistence on self-determination is characteristic of most of the older women and younger men we've interviewed. This characteristic is essential if they are to confront and overcome the prejudice with which their relationship will be met.

3 •

GOING PUBLIC

An older woman/younger man couple begins to feel pressure as soon as they tell people who are important to them that their relationship is becoming serious. Family, friends, and co-workers express their disapproval of the relationship in a multitude of ways, although total rejection is rare. As a rule, outsiders are likely to be more uncomfortable with the relationship than with the couple as individuals. Discomfort generally shows itself in pointed questions or doubtful comments about the suitability of the situation.

Forty-six-year-old Susan Howard has lived for five years with thirty-one-year-old Peter Levin. She told us about an incident with Peter's family that left both of them alternately puzzled, annoyed, and amused. Early in their relationship, Susan and Peter went to a family wedding. An aunt of Peter's noticed Susan and asked who she was. The aunt was informed that Susan was the woman Peter lived with. The aunt shook her head. "Oh, no, Peter lives with a much older woman. I want to know who that pretty girl with the big brown eyes is." Peter's aunt was assured that the pretty girl with the big brown eyes was indeed Susan, the older woman in Peter's life. The aunt stared at Susan disapprovingly. "Well," she finally said, "it won't work out. She's much too old for him."

Appearances notwithstanding, reactions to the older woman/younger man relationship often depend on certain fixed ideas about the suitability of who should be with whom.

Many family members — parents, children, and relatives — initially view the relationship with suspicion. Their attitude largely derives from a genuine concern for the member of the family who is involved in the older woman/younger man relationship. They are worried about what they see as a problem. They would probably have the same worries about any pairing that departed from ordinary social expectations, such as a marriage between people from different religions or races. They are afraid that the couple will be subject to severe disapproval. They are afraid, as well, that the relationship will break up and the person they care about will be hurt. In addition, they are afraid for the family's reputation. The family is simultaneously convinced that the relationship won't last and equally terrified that it might.

Generally, families react to some degree upon hearing that one of their own is involved with a woman who is older or a man who is younger. Often the reaction is minor; usually it is temporary. For instance, Mr. and Ms. Jeff and Barbara Courtney-Fein are not conventional in the way they chose to do their lives or their marriage, but their parents' initial response to their older woman/younger man relationship was fairly typical. Barbara commented, "I think my father is kind of accepting of it at this point, but he certainly made mention of it on a number of occasions. Early in the relationship he said to me, 'You realize you're older than he is; in a few years he might be attracted to women younger than you.' I disagreed with him."

Jeff added, 'My mother said things like 'She's not the woman for you. You're not supposed to be with a woman older than you.' My mother was very concerned about the age thing. She just didn't like it at all."

Jeff's mother and Barbara's father initially resisted the marriage. Interestingly enough, the parents did not bring up the difference in religious backgrounds or the difference in socioeconomic backgrounds. Simply because Barbara was eight years older than Jeff, the more traditional objections to marriage were overlooked.

While all parents may not react overtly, there is generally a hint of frost in the air as the family adjusts to the older woman/younger man relationship. When we asked one woman how her relatives responded to her fifteen-year-younger lover, she replied, "With great caution!" Tina Carey, a forty-seven-year-old business executive, told us, "I haven't had any direct kind of reaction or comment from my family about David's being eleven years younger. Just a vague atmosphere of disapproval from my mother. We eat dinner at my mother's about once a week. What it is, is that she never asks David to come to dinner unless I ask if David can come."

All families behave somewhat peculiarly upon meeting a prospective in-law or a new romance. The person being introduced is uneasy about being inspected. The family is equally nervous about what the newcomer will think of them. In the case of the older woman/younger man relationship, the natural nervousness of both the family and the future in-law is often intensified by the unusual nature of the relationship.

Gail, thirty-eight, married to Steve, twenty-six, talked about how she felt when she first met Steve's family.

"The only time I ever got any really intense feeling of disapproval about our ages was during that initial meeting when they were questioning me. It was nothing anybody ever said, but their body language and some of their gestures indicated a sort of shock followed by disapproval. I felt like a carcass on the desert with all these birds swarming down to pick my bones. I was surrounded and bombarded by all these incredible questions about myself, who I was and what I'd been doing."

Almost no one that we have interviewed seems to have escaped that initial period of suspicion. In most situations, the general feeling of distrust eventually disappeared, but a number of people have confided that a relative or two is still holding out.

Sometimes family disapproval is more than tinged with disappointment. A young minister, who was considering marriage to a woman thirteen years older than he, said that his father's only comment about his decision was "Now, you'll never get to be a bishop!"

In the early stages of the relationship family members often assume that the couple is not facing the realities of life. Their comments reflect those anxieties. Susan Howard, forty-six, told us about a discussion with her stepsister which took place after she and Peter, then thirty-one, had been together for about a year.

"My stepsister was very concerned about my being hurt. She saw the relationship as temporary at best; she was worried that I might take it as more than an affair and wind up devastated when Peter left me for a younger woman. I think many people in my life waited to see whether it was going to last before they committed themselves to caring about Peter and accepting us as a couple."

Family members and friends often voiced their fears that the woman would eventually be left by the younger man for a younger woman, and that their loved person might be badly hurt. A variation on the theme was occasionally mentioned by members of the man's family. They thought that for the older, supposedly more sophisticated, woman, a relationship with a younger man might be merely a short-term episode in her life. After a while the older woman would naturally leave the younger man and move on to someone her own age who would be a more suitable partner. Some family members felt very strongly at the beginning of the relationship that their sons and brothers, sisters and daughters were just a temporary novelty who would soon be tossed aside.

A number of the women we interviewed had previously been married to men of achievement and wealth. Other women we talked to had acquired a certain position in the world through their own independent efforts. One of the questions that frequently arose had to do with differences in the couple's social, economic, and professional status. A well-to-do divorcée from Beverly Hills explained how that issue affected her.

"My mother, although she doesn't like to admit it, was worried about my younger man's ability to give me the life-style that I had been used to. My ex-husband is a wealthy film producer. He socializes with other successful, well-known people. I think my mother was concerned about three things; my social standing, my financial welfare, and whether I might not soon be bored with a younger, less successful man."

A woman in our society has been brought up to define herself through her man — her husband, boss, or boyfriend. It is very difficult, even a decade into the women's movement, for her to stop judging herself by her mate's accomplishments. Other women, in particular, tend to evaluate her worth by her mate's social standing. This is a subtle issue and one that directly affects how the outsider perceives the older woman/younger man relationship.

For the achievement-oriented American, when an older woman chooses a younger man for a partner, it looks as if she is choosing a social inferior. For all of their natterings about equality, Americans are snobs. Older woman/younger man relationships appear to snub the value system, and therefore raise social hackles. Family members, in particular, react to what seems to be a socially inappropriate bonding.

A relative sometimes feels that a sister, daughter, or even mother may not be getting the man to whom she is entitled by virtue of age or social position. Family members also have a secondary fear. By involving herself in this relationship, the older woman may actually lose the status she has acquired through a previous marriage.

And what about the younger man? What kind of social discomfort will he or his family have to suffer? Will there be questions about his immaturity, need for a mother, or other neurotic tendencies? There probably will. Men in relationships with older women are definitely suspect. Some men have told us that they have been accused of social climbing, sexual exploitation, or wanting to embarrass their families by looking to the rest of the world like gigolos.

Thirty-one-year-old Peter Levin recalls trying to figure out how to break the news to his parents that at twenty-six he was seriously involved with a forty-one-year-old woman who had three teenaged children.

"I come from a conventionally Jewish family who live in the San Fernando Valley section of Los Angeles. In my student days at U.C.L.A. I lived for three years with a lady of Mexican-American descent. Neither my family nor hers was especially thrilled by the relationship. After we broke up, I fell in love with a lady who was a Lebanese Catholic radical feminist. My parents never said much, but I could tell they weren't too excited by her either. Then I met Susan. When I told my parents I was serious about her, my mother had that funny look on her face again and I blurted out, 'But it's okay, Ma, she's Jewish!' "

However, after a period of bewilderment most family members respond very positively. As it becomes obvious that the people in these relationships are very good for each other, that they are sincere in their commitment to each other, parents and siblings relax and welcome the new in-law into their midst.

For a few couples it has not been that easy. Parents, in particular, can have strenuous objections to the relationship. Even in the face of all evidence that the couple is psychologically and socially well matched, that their lives together are working out well, the parents may continue to ignore the positive aspects of the relationship. Their children are not living up to proper social expectations and the parents feel betrayed or even disgraced. Sometimes, they continue to feel that way for months or even years.

Shoshana Halevi, thirty-five, and Robbie Wise, twenty-three, have experienced enormous resistance to their relationship from Robbie's parents. The situation is particularly painful in that Shoshana was a close friend of Robbie's family before she actually met him. His parents feel that by becoming seriously involved with their son, she has betrayed the friendship. When we first interviewed them, Robbie's parents were not speaking to Shoshana nor acknowledging her as Robbie's wife.

Shoshana was born and grew up in Israel. She has a twelve-year-old son by a previous marriage. After her divorce, at the age of thirty, Shoshana reentered the university in addition to working and taking care of her child. During this period Robbie's family, who are Americans, moved to Israel and became neighbors of Shoshana's. Shoshana and the Wises became very close friends. She was treated like a member of the family. In particular, Robbie's father admired her because of her determination to get her university degree and make something of herself.

By the time Robbie came to Israel to visit his family, Shoshana had heard so much about him that she felt she knew him. They immediately liked each other. Shortly after their meeting they began an affair. One night they had a long talk about how their relationship couldn't possibly work out because of the age difference. By the end of that conversation they realized that they were very much in love. But until Robbie left Israel neither of them ever considered a permanent relationship.

After Robbie went back to the United States he and Shoshana wrote to each other. Gradually they came to the conclusion that each meant too much to the other to give up the relationship. They decided that Shoshana would come to the United States and that they would get married.

The morning before Shoshana was to leave for the United States, Robbie called his parents and told them that he and Shoshana were planning to be married. Shoshana went to the Wise apartment later that day to say good-bye. She told us: "When I entered the house I felt you could cut the atmosphere with a knife. I kind of suspected what it was. I asked Mr. Wise, 'What worries you?' He said, 'Oh, problems.' I said, 'With the children?' and he said, 'In a way.' I couldn't make him talk frankly. All the love and affection and appreciation for what I was going through to get through school, all that was gone. The only thing he said to me was that it wasn't ethical, that I should marry my own age."

Robbie talked about his father's reaction to the relationship: "I wanted to confront my father, so I wrote to him. I tried to get at what he really felt, what were the points he wanted to make, how, exactly, was he against the relationship. The only thing he had ever actually said was, 'What about later on . . . what about ten, fifteen years from now?' As if we hadn't thought about that, talked about it, and decided that nobody can tell you what's going to happen fifteen years from now."

Although Robbie wrote several times asking for his father's reasons for being against the marriage, Mr. Wise never wrote an answer. Instead, Robbie's parents continued to correspond with Robbie as if Shoshana weren't there. It took over a year for them to recognize Shoshana's presence in Robbie's life and accept her as his wife. But even though the Wises have officially accepted Shoshana as their daughter-in-law, they have not been able to offer her the warm, close friendship that they originally shared.

Although many couples have talked about varying levels of resistance that they encountered from their families, a few people have told us that their families welcomed the older woman or the younger man as though nothing was out of the ordinary.

Mary Bayer, forty-one, married to Mike Bayer, twenty-six, told us that her mother-in-law accepted her with total enthusiasm. We called Anita Bayer and asked for an interview. She was more than happy to talk to us and excited by the opportunity to air her views on her son's marriage to an older woman.

As the tape recorder clicked on, Anita launched into a description of the changes in Mike that she attributes to his relationship with Mary.

"Mike is much more serious; he's much more aware. I think he has grown enormously since he has been married; it's such a pleasure to be with him. He had this hypertense thing going all the time. Now he's happy, he's relaxed; he knows where he's going and what it's all about. Mary was probably one of the best things that ever happened to him."

Does Anita have any misgivings about her twenty-six-year-old being married to a forty-one-year-old woman with three grown sons?

"I have no worries about the relationship. However, I am very concerned about Mary having a child at this time in her life. One comment made by my friends scared the hell out of me. Like, if somebody has a baby at that age, they don't come out normal. But Mary went through the tests at U.C.L.A. and at least she didn't have to worry about the baby being okay. But besides that, I don't think any woman who has raised three sons should have to go through that again. Hey, she's ready to go out and do her own thing with Mike and here she is with a baby."

"And how about their physical appearance together?" we asked Anita. "Is the age difference obvious? Does it embarrass you?" Anita smiled. "I never knew her age the first month and a half they were together because she looks like a child. I imagined her to be about twenty-four or twenty-five at the most. Mike does not look twenty-six; he could pass for thirty. So, no, there's no obvious age difference. And if there were, it wouldn't bother me. Look at all the couples who are the same age where the woman looks much older than the man. Appearance is not that important. I think Mary and Mike meet each other's needs perfectly."

Anita and Larry Bayer are one set of parents who were delighted with their daughter-in-law from the beginning. They really liked Mary and were pleased by Mike's decision to marry her. The Bayers represent one extreme of parental reaction to the older woman/younger man relationship and the Wises represent the other. The change in the Wise family's attitude toward Shoshana occurred solely because she and Robbie wanted to marry.

There is no doubt that most families are distrustful of the

older woman/younger man relationship. Sometimes friends have the same reaction. Friends, however, tend to accept these relationships with more ease than families do. Since a lot of the people we've interviewed are somewhat unconventional, it follows that their friends would be more accepting of an unorthodox relationship. However, some people who thought they knew a great deal about their friends, particularly long-term friends, experienced some surprising reactions.

Anita Bayer mentioned that practically all of her friends were very much upset by her son's marriage and felt that it didn't have a chance. We wondered if Anita could remember any of the questions that she and her husband were asked.

"Sure, I do," she said. "I think I can tell you verbatim. 'Do you realize that in ten years he's going to be thirty-four and she is going to be forty-nine?' I said, 'Yes, I do!' And then, 'He's still very young; he doesn't have the maturity that she has,' and I said, 'Well, that's good, at least one person has the maturity.' Oh, yes, the baby! 'Do you realize that when the baby is ten years old, she's going to be forty-nine?' I said, 'I'm over forty-nine and I could handle a ten-year-old child right now!' There was kind of a personal involvement; I got angry at one point. There's nothing like being bored to death by redundancy; nothing worse than to know exactly what someone is going to tell you, to the point where you just want to say, shut up, I've heard it. There's kind of an intellectual insult that accompanies all of this because obviously haven't I thought of all these things too?

"However," Anita concluded, "I've seen so many marvelous marriages go down the drain that I know the old formula doesn't necessarily work. It's not always successful, you know — the same age, religion, money — you can throw them all out because I've seen the perfect combinations prove to be the most destructive relationships."

The same questions; the same comments. Most of the people we've interviewed have listened to the point of tedium and have felt the implied insult. "She's too old for him; he's too young for her; what's the point of this marriage?" Behind this kind of comment is a constant unspoken message. "Do you really expect us, your friends, to freely endorse a situation that openly defies social tradition?"

The late Theodora Kroeber-Quinn married artist John Quinn, twenty-nine, when she was seventy-three years old. In the article mentioned in Chapter 2, Dr. Kroeber-Quinn discussed the older woman/younger man marriage from an anthropological point of view. She describes the behavior of both men and women toward the couple, as she has observed it:

"How do the men react to a reverse marriage in which the wife is old? Promptly. Negatively. Denunciatorily. Moralistically. Either the woman is an old fool who is being taken by a young scoundrel, or both man and wife are, quite simply, beyond the pale. Surely the old woman does not expect her friends to accept this indecently young man? . . . and what stance toward the young man? Fatherly? Patronizingly at ease? Jolly? . . . Meanwhile, why, the man asks himself, are the women so damned unconcerned? To all appearances, so acquiescent, ruminative? So intrigued? So preoccupied in quietly, coolly, openly sizing up the young husband? It can't be they are fantasizing young lovers of their own? Well, of course, it can. They do."[1]

Older woman/younger man relationships can sometimes be as much of a problem for the couple's friends as they are for the couple. People are often threatened by anything that is out of the ordinary. Eventually, most people are able to adjust to the couple in which the woman is older than the man. Some people, however, just never get used to the idea and remain acutely uncomfortable in the presence of the couple.

A few people won't deal with it at all and abandon the offending friend.

Society has never really sanctioned the older woman/ younger man relationship. Possibly it never will. Inevitably both the couple and their friends will experience discomfort in social situations, particularly at those levels of society where the traditions of the culture are most rigorously observed.

Andrea Graham, forty-six, divorced, has lived in Beverly Hills for twenty years. She talks about her friends' response to her divorce from her film-producer husband, and to her subsequent relationship with free-lance writer Mel Brenner, thirty-one: "I met Mel right around the time of my separation from my ex-husband. It was a very confusing period and I think a lot of my friends felt that my relationship with Mel was a fling; people going through divorces can behave strangely. A lot of people who I had thought were my friends disappeared out of my life after Martin and I separated. For a long time I wasn't sure whether it was because I was getting divorced, losing a husband who had status that I don't have, or taking up with a man who was fifteen years my junior. I guess I could have been dropped for any one of those reasons. I'll never know for sure.

"Anyway, for a long time nobody knew what to do with us. We didn't say we were going to get married and we didn't say it was going to be forever. For a while we weren't sure about anything. It was good; we were going to let it go on, and it looked like it could last for quite a long time. Generally, my friends who remained friends had a positive attitude toward me and Mel; but sometimes I could feel bubbles of disapproval underneath, and occasionally criticism would erupt. I could see how they could be concerned about us. If I had seen somebody in a similar situation, before my experience with Mel, I might have been very concerned for them.

Still, I was very hurt whenever friends withheld acceptance of Mel as my significant person or referred to our relationship as temporary. And they often did both."

Andrea comes from a social background where money and professional achievement have a great deal to do with social acceptance. Mel, being younger, was not at that level of accomplishment. Because professional and social status are so important in Andrea's world, none of her friends wanted to believe her relationship with Mel was serious. It took quite a bit of time for Mel and Andrea to be accepted as a couple by Andrea's social peers.

Mel Brenner looks back on that period somewhat ruefully: "I couldn't at the time perceive that we were a problem. But now I know we were a problem in some people's minds. They thought of us as a label: older, younger, whatever. I never thought about it myself until someone reminded me of it, usually by ignoring me."

One of the ways that outsiders cope with unorthodox relationships is by not recognizing the existence of the partner who is not their personal friend. It is not uncommon for the younger man to be socially ignored. After observing the basic amenities of introduction, the older woman's friends often simply walk away. Those friends of the older woman who feel they must make more of a gesture often talk to the man in the manner usually reserved for obscure younger cousins. And the situation works in reverse.

The younger man's friends can be intimidated by the older woman, particularly if she has money and status of her own. Sometimes it is a question of generational differences. The younger man's friends may simply not trust anyone over thirty. Quietly and efficiently, either the older woman or the younger man can be excluded from the conversation of the social group.

Mel is usually a warm, easygoing person, but his eyes

glitter with anger as he says, "Sometimes I got so frustrated with some of Andrea's closest friends that I blew up. Actually, it was rather childish of me, but, at least, from then on, they knew I was there."

Andrea added thoughtfully, "Early in our relationship Mel and I were at a party of his old college buddies. They were talking about the things they had done and shared in the radical sixties. Every time I made a comment they would stare at me politely and then go on with the conversation as if I wasn't there. I finally got so fed up that I just got up and left the party. I walked for two hours, burning with anger and embarrassment, and came back just as the party was breaking up. Nobody actually said anything, but Mel's friends made a point of coming up to say good-bye and telling me how much they had enjoyed meeting me."

For most of us, there is a certain amount of socializing that is a part of working. Usually, a number of co-workers are also friends. Like the rest of one's friends, some fellow employees may be worried about the consequences of choosing an older female or younger male partner. Some of them fear that jobs or promotions might be in jeopardy.

Susan Howard, author and college professor, told us: "There is a standing joke among teachers that a charge of moral turpitude is really the only way to ever get anyone fired once they have tenure. One of my male colleagues was seriously worried about how administrative knowledge of my relationship might affect my professional standing. I found it amusing, and revealing, that he was far more concerned about Peter's age than he was about our living together without being married."

Liz Stefano, a thirty-eight-year-old psychologist married for three years to a man ten years her junior, said, "Nobody at work ever said to me, 'Are you sure you're doing the right thing?' My impression was that everyone just accepted us. My husband, Paul, who works for a utility company, sees it a little differently. He was aware that he was being indirectly questioned by his friends at work. He remembers getting a lot of quizzical looks and surprised noises from them."

Liz Stefano is not particularly concerned about what her friends might think of Paul and herself as a couple. However, she is very intrigued by the reactions of strangers. She was talking to a sixteen-year-old girl at a party and the girl asked who her husband was. Liz pointed at Paul. The girl's first reaction was disbelief. "You two are married?" Then quick recovery. "That's so wonderful!" the teenager gushed. "He must be a lot older than I thought he was."

Absolute strangers sometimes exhibit a curious antagonism when encountering a relationship in which the woman looks older than the man. Too often for her comfort, the woman is asked if the man is her son. We wonder a lot about this question. If the age difference is so obvious, why doesn't anybody ever ask if the young man is her brother? Mary Jo and Paul, who have been living together for three years, have a twenty-two-year age difference. When they were apartment hunting, they got chilly looks and hostile questions. They decided to introduce themselves as sister and brother and the atmosphere grew decidedly warmer.

In a number of older woman/younger man relationships, the man does look obviously younger than the woman, but it's rare that he actually looks young enough to be her son. Something is definitely going on within the person who asks if the man is the woman's son. Usually the physical evidence isn't that clear.

We think that people are initially confused by these relationships. They are experiencing something that is not as it should be. An unusual situation can often produce anger in people, simply because they don't know how to deal with the unexpected. The normal social signals are all mixed up. People literally don't know what to do, so they leak hostility.

For example, Miriam, nineteen years older than her husband, Louis, is a marriage and family counselor who is trained to look for behavioral responses. She talks about what happens when they go shopping or into a restaurant: "Everyone is slightly uncomfortable. They like us as people but they're really not sure how to react to us. It's really funny to watch the reactions of the sales clerks because they can't quite figure it out. Now, is he a gigolo and she's buying clothes for him, or is it his mother who's coming along because he doesn't have a girlfriend and he doesn't have good taste? So, they're really uncomfortable. You see it in their faces, they hesitate, they don't know how to address you, they don't know whether to ask me for an opinion or ask him for an opinion; it's very definitely observable to the person who knows what to look for."

Barry and Jenna Trenton have had their own unique experience with public disapproval of their mariage. Barry, the twenty-eight-year-old Englishman, was in the process of filing for immigration papers when he and fifty-four-year-old Jenna decided to get married. With some heat, Jenna described what she went through with the United States Immigration Service: "They hassled me, and they have got exactly the points to hassle me on. They had me so upset the first time we went through it. They interviewed us separately; they said I was a secretary and was being paid for this. They brought in a large pile of folders and said, 'We would like to invite you to come back alone; we have all of these horror stories of what has happened to nice ladies like you married to opportunistic young men. If you'd like to come back alone you can read all of these.' And they called me after the interview and said, 'We felt impelled to ask you to look around because generally in these situations we find a young girl somewhere in the background.' I was upset when they said that to me. I'm sure it triggered some of my fears. You don't see any young girls in the background, but you wonder if maybe you should start looking for them. I didn't know what to do with it. Finally, it just wore out, but it was certainly upsetting."

We asked Barry if there had been any indignities in his interviews with the Immigration Service. Barry laughed.

"One question they asked me was 'How do you feel about it? Are you worried about it at all, the age difference?' I said, 'Well, no, it doesn't worry me.' And they said, 'Well, does it worry anybody?' And I said, 'Yes, it sure as hell worries my mother a lot.' But no, the Immigration Service didn't give me anywhere near as much trouble as they gave Jenna."

Jenna reflected for a moment and then said fiercely: "They gave me a lot more trouble. They wanted to know under what circumstances we had decided to get married. Did his lawyer pay me, did Barry pay me? It just went on and on, and on. One of them put his hand on my shoulder and said, 'A nice lady like you; I hate to see this happen to nice ladies.' At that point I really wanted to tell him I had taken advantage of more young boys . . ."

Most of the people we have talked to have felt that the woman in the older woman/younger man relationship experiences more pressure to conform than the man. Perhaps people feel that since she is older she should know better than to agree to an unsuitable relationship. If she decides to marry a much younger man, a woman's maturity is suspect; her sanity may even be questioned. In the case of Jenna Trenton, her status in her own profession was humiliatingly tossed aside: "They insisted I was a secretary and was being paid for this." The hostility and fear toward nonconforming behavior tends, in some people, to come out under the guise of protectiveness and concern for the woman's well-being.

Fears about older woman/younger man relationships can

be legitimate. They are usually based on the reality that the going will not be totally smooth for the older woman and the younger man who are determined to get on with their relationship. But a negative attitude from the people whom one loves and trusts is particularly hard to take when the couple is in the position of wanting all the support they can get for their relationship.

The couple involved in an older woman/younger man relationship will have enough personal fears about that relationship to occupy them full-time without carrying the additional burden of the projected fantasies of others. The men and women who are willing to risk such a relationship are struggling intensely with their own doubts. Long before the relationship is made public, they have considered the issues raised by others. The thing for older woman/younger man couples to remember, however, is that most of the resistance from family and friends stems from real concern.

A forty-five-year-old widow who was planning to marry a thirty-two-year-old man was dismayed to discover that her thirty-year-old son-in-law, with whom she was very close, was extremely upset by the idea of the marriage. The woman was wise enough to realize that her son-in-law had very protective feelings about her. Since the death of her husband, he had felt responsible for her care. She took the time to express her appreciation for his concern and agreed that there was considerable risk in her choice. She then explained to him that this was what she had decided to do with her life and that her son-in-law's support, if he felt he could give it, would be very valuable to her. This struck us as being an effective way of dealing with the fears of other people.

Acknowledging the concern and discomfort of the others who care and giving them time to adjust to a rather unexpected set of circumstances is a realistic way of handling the situation. Gossip and the occasional snide remark are inevitable. The older woman/younger man couple has to learn to live with some social tension, to share and laugh at it, and take most of it with a large grain of salt.

Whether it's family, friends, salespersons, waitresses, or the milkman, people do have a startled reaction to these relationships. Even when approval is given, it can take a downright peculiar form. For instance, Susan Howard's twice-widowed mother said to her with a sigh, "Well, at least you won't outlive Peter; there's comfort in that."

People who involve themselves in older woman/younger man relationships must accept the fact that others may react to them unfavorably. It helps if they understand that there is not much point in using a great deal of effort to get other people to accept the relationship immediately. Time and familiarity will take care of most of that problem. The major part of one's energy, strength, and persistence needs to be saved for dealing with one's own fears about embarking on this kind of relationship.

4 ·

PRIVATE FEARS

ON THE DAY OF HER WEDDING TO PAUL STEFANO, LIZ Miller stood in front of a full-length mirror. She wore a pale yellow floor-length gown. A yellow rose in her dark brown hair gave her a slightly Latin look. The yellow roses nestled below her full breasts took the place of a bouquet. At thirty-five she felt prettier than she had ever felt in her life. All the parts of her life were going well — career, friends, and Paul.

But as she waited for their guests to arrive, Liz felt her body tensing in fear. She had a drink with Paul in order to relax. It half worked. She felt looser on the outside, but the tension only burrowed deeper inside. As a psychologist Liz knew that her fears were natural. She was frightened by the prospect of entering a second marriage. She was afraid of making a mistake; she was afraid of committing herself to Paul; she was afraid of allowing herself to need Paul when she had worked for years to develop an independent life. And on top of all that, she was afraid because she was doing something unusual. She was marrying a man who was ten years younger.

The wedding went perfectly. Surrounded by their dearest friends, Paul and Liz pledged their love and friendship. Liz enjoyed the day of celebration, pushing her fears to the farthest corner of her mind. After all, it was not a mistake to marry Paul. They had lived together successfully for nearly a year and it had been an exciting time for them.

Liz described her feelings to us as well as their consequences. "On top of the usual scariness about a second marriage, I had all the typical fears about getting old while Paul just got better. I'm thirty-five and my hair is graying. In another ten years it'll be half gray. The character lines in my face will become wrinkles. As I get older how will he react to my looking middle-aged? Will I still be beautiful in his eyes? I guess I was scared because I didn't know the answers to all those questions. I was taking a big risk, walking into the unknown. I felt cold and disconnected, as though all the blood was drained out of my body.

"For a week following the wedding I felt anxious. Even though I had made the decision to go ahead, somewhere inside me the battle was still raging. Fear led to tension and tension took hold of my body. I got a pinched nerve in my neck and was flat on my back for ten days."

Liz Stefano's intense anxiety about marrying Paul was typical of the fears of an older woman committing herself to a younger man, even though the symptoms are ordinarily not so severe. Since the marriage ceremony symbolized the decision to commit herself to the relationship, the wedding itself brought back fears that she thought she had already put behind her.

There are many aspects of the older woman/younger man relationship that are genuinely frightening. Both women and men can be drastically affected by anxiety about the risks they are taking, to the point where the relationship may break up. Those who remain together must find means of coping with these fears.

One prevalent fear grows out of uncertainty about what will happen when the woman shows signs of physical aging. The women worry more than the men do. Considering the great emphasis on youth in our society, this is not surprising.

A thirty-five-year-old artist told us, "Right now I'm remembering getting up at Jerry's house after spending the night there, going in the bathroom and looking in the mirror with no makeup on. I looked like an old hag. I walked back in the room and there was this beautiful young boy lying in the bed, firm rear end and not a wrinkle. I couldn't lie there with him and have him look at me. I sort of hid my face because I felt so old and ugly and he was so young and beautiful. Men age, but I think women age a lot faster. In ten years, when I am forty-five, he will still be young and I will be old. I couldn't bear the thought of it, So I gave Jerry up to save myself from hurt in the future."

A petite forty-one-year-old nursery school teacher described her feelings of insecurity about her twenty-eight-year-old boyfriend. "I worried about looking much older and I talked about it. I had fantasies that some younger woman would come and take him and I wouldn't have a chance. That worried me a lot. I got reassurance from him but it didn't matter. I felt somehow that it couldn't last because I was that much older. I can remember going to visit my boyfriend's sister. His father was there and the whole family. I thought, 'Oh my God, they're going to drop dead. Here comes this older woman.' Even though I had no sense of their disapproving, I still was afraid."

And from a thirty-six-year-old public health administrator about dating younger men: "I think aging will always be an issue for me. There's always going to be a question in my mind, no matter how much I'm reassured. Because of my own feelings of insecurity, it will be scarier for me. When I'm with a guy my own age, I feel desirable and like a young chick. I feel really good. I am scared with a young guy, even though he may say all the right words."

Each of these comments emphasizes fear of physical aging in connection with the relationship. Reassurance from the young man doesn't really help when the woman's fear is so strong. For the three women quoted above, anxiety about growing older precludes a relationship with a younger man. Their fears are not a result of anything that has actually happened. They are part of these women's own internal processes, a personal fear of aging. As one of the women specifically said, "Because of my own feelings of insecurity, it [a relationship with a younger man] will be scarier for me."

If a woman's feeling of insecurity about her own aging is so intense, a relationship with a younger man is not a good idea for her. A woman in this kind of relationship must have efficient ways of dealing with her fears about physical aging.

While women, more than their mates, worry about the potential loss of physical beauty, both partners are concerned about the degeneration of health.

"I sometimes wonder whether I'll be able to keep up with Louis' pace of physical activity," says fifty-five-year-old Miriam, whose husband is nineteen years younger.

"I'm afraid I might get seriously sick and he'd have to take care of me." A sixty-two-year-old factory assembler expressed fears of being dependent on her fifty-one-year-old husband.

Barry Trenton, twenty-eight, told us his greatest worry regarding his wife, Jenna, fifty-four. "One of my major fears is what do I do in twenty years when Jenna will be seventy-five. Knowing Jenna, she will probably still be running all over the place. But when I'm in my mid- or late forties, it's possible that either Jenna will be dead or I'll be taking care of her. At the moment it's not the loss that's worrying me; it's what the hell am I going to do? Will I put her in a home or nursemaid her? Any couple might have this problem, but I'll have to deal with it at forty-eight whereas most people have to deal with it at the age of seventy."

Barry's fears about Jenna's growing old are genuine, as are all the other fears our interviewees expressed. If no way is found to deal with such fears, the couple may, as we have seen, break up. Let's take a look at some of the other fears common to older women/younger men couples. Then we'll discuss how couples who have stayed together have managed to overcome them.

Of all the fears expressed, the fear of being left for a younger woman was the one most often mentioned to us. Women heard it from their friends and relatives. Over and over this point is repeated. Many women told us that this idea worried them mostly at the beginning of the relationship.

Mary Bayer, forty-one, married to Mike, twenty-six, says, "When I first met him, I thought he would probably find somebody younger and leave me for that person. I don't have those feelings anymore. I can't really say that I'm that afraid of the future right now."

A thirty-four-year-old woman told us, "Yes, that's very much in the back of my mind. If not a younger woman, he will leave me for another woman, period. I do have those insecurities. But I'm not sure whether it's because my boyfriend is younger or because it's happened to me before. The fact that he is younger makes it worse."

A woman fears being left for many valid reasons. Socially, she is not supposed to initiate new relationships with men. A divorced woman usually has to take almost complete responsibility for her children's care. If she is older, entering the job market is difficult. She is sometimes at the level of a twenty-year-old in terms of her ability to handle finances.

In addition, women are raised to believe they need the protection of a male. They feel vulnerable to the sexual advances of men when they begin to date again and they are afraid of coping in the single world, a world where youth and beauty have a high priority. For all these reasons women develop obsessive fears concerning their ability to hold onto their men. Women who are involved with younger men have to cope with all their normal fears of abandonment, plus the possibility of being rejected simply because they are older than their men.

A woman's fear of being left is most noticeable during the period of deepening commitment. In this period not enough time has passed to ensure the stability of the relationship. Trust will grow only over time as the older woman experiences the man's keeping the agreements they have made together.

We want to point out that no one ever says to the young man, "Aren't you afraid she will leave you for a man her age, an older man, or an even younger man?" Yet this is a real worry for several of the younger men we've interviewed. They are aware of the older woman's accomplishments and of her desirability to other men. The younger man may feel some insecurity because of his own lack of sophistication or financial success.

When Mary Bayer told her husband that she got nervous if she saw him looking at other women, Mike said to her: "Haven't you ever thought that I might be afraid you'd leave me for a successful executive type? There are Cary Grants out there with twenty-five suits in their closets. They know just what to say and just how to act. I have fears, too."

Several younger men said they were afraid they might leave

their mates for another woman, but not necessarily a younger woman. Thirty-one-year-old Peter Levin describes his feelings: "Sometimes I wonder if I am tricking myself about not being into the 'I-need-young-new-bodies-all-the-time-to-make-sex-exciting' syndrome that is so popular in American society. A part of me, in my fantasies occasionally, gets off on that attitude. Most of me, particularly my serious 'adult' self, is revolted by that stuff. Will I change into that attitude against my serious wishes? My feeling is, if I do, I hope Susan leaves me.

"My fear about growing older is not related to Susan. She'll always be a gorgeous lady, one of those who age with delicate grace. My fear is that when *I* am over forty, will I turn into an overly macho, insecure, middle-ager who has to prove his manhood through inane sexual, athletic, or monetary exploits? This is the script which is written for the majority of American men in that age group, and perhaps my relationship with Susan is due partly to my wish to write a new script for myself."

Some women fear that the younger man may want her only for her money or for the favors she can do for him.

When the word gets out that a younger man is about to marry an older woman, it often happens that someone will say, "She must have a lot of money." The implication is that the only attraction the older woman has left is her money, her status, or her power to help the young man get ahead.

There is no question that wealthy women are sometimes financially exploited by younger men. They are also exploited by men their own age. A number of the women we interviewed are financially better off than the men. They are willing to share with the man but not support him. Those women we talked to who were worried about the possibility of being used by younger men usually took some kind of action to protect themselves, mostly in the form of legal agreements about money. The financial arrangements of older women/younger men couples are often not conventional.

Jenna Trenton, fifty-four, earns three times as much as her husband, Barry, twenty-eight years old. This fact no longer bothers her, but there was a time when she was afraid to trust Barry's love for her. She wondered if he cared enough about her to support her. She decided to test her fear and Barry, too. Shortly after their marriage they moved from the East Coast to the West Coast. Jenna decided privately she would not get a job for six months to see what Barry would do. All their money ran out. Barry finally found a job. Jenna continued to avoid finding one. Barry supported them both for quite a while and eventually Jenna went back to work.

Afraid of being used, Jenna needed to check out Barry's willingness to support her in order to rid herself of her fear. We wish that more women with money of their own would be willing to test directly the goodwill of their partners instead of living with the kind of suspicion that will eventually corrode the relationship.

Another feeling expressed by the women and men we interviewed was the fear of disapproval. They were worried that disapproval would take the form of ridicule. Fear of disapproval and ridicule is entirely realistic. People talk disparagingly about older woman/younger man couples. The women are called dirty old ladies or cradle-snatchers. The men are thought to be henpecked, or, still worse, emotionally disturbed.

Liz Stefano witnessed this vignette: "I saw an older woman and a handsome young man go through the supermarket checkout counter together. When they walked away, the checker and bagger, both young women, glanced at each other knowingly. With a look of pure disgust, the checker said, 'Did you see *that*?' The bagger answered, 'Yeah, I just hate to see old women with young men.' "

Older woman/younger man couples are ridiculed both openly and behind their backs. The ways they are ridiculed are varied. The more direct methods are straight criticism and teasing. Tom told us that his nineteen-year-old girlfriend broke up with him because she was embarrassed by her friends' teasing. He was sixteen at the time. His girlfriend was told, "Don't rock the cradle." Somehow her friends combined two old sayings, "Don't rock the boat" and "Don't rob the cradle." In other words, do conform and do date someone your own age.

Some women with younger husbands have been asked, "Is he your son?" This particular question is usually asked by a stranger, usually a man. The man is usually the same age or older than the woman. We suggest that this question is an expression of the man's disapproval of the situation. He is probably angry at seeing a woman connected to a younger man with whom he feels he can't compete.

Liz Stefano told us how these experiences affect her: "I used to be afraid when we were in public. Twice a man I didn't know has said to me, 'Is that your son?' Each time it angered me and hurt my feelings. Each time it was when Paul was not nearby. (No one has ever said to Paul, 'Is that your mother?') I'm not scared of it anymore. I expect that it will occasionally happen. I'm more prepared now."

Women tell us these remarks don't occur often, but when they do, they sting. However, their effect gets less and less powerful as time goes by.

In the beginning of older woman/younger man relationships, it is more common for the woman to fear the opinions of other people. But one thirty-two-year-old man told us of taking his new girlfriend, twelve years older than he, to a favorite restaurant for dinner. As they were standing in the foyer waiting to be seated, the younger man suddenly panicked. "I was in a cold sweat," he said. "I thought people were staring at us. I was scared about what people would think of me. I started looking for a good reason to get out of there. Then, as suddenly as it started, my panic was gone. I was just introducing my new lady to my favorite restaurant. Fortunately," the man concluded, "it never happened again or I would have seriously considered not going on with the relationship."

Neither men nor women are exempt from fear of social criticism. Underlying the fear of criticism is the fear of abandonment. We imagine that if we are too independent of others they will turn away from us. Or if we behave too differently from the way other people do, we will end up alone. This fear has a realistic base. Some people *will* turn away from nonconforming behavior. The marriage of an older woman and a younger man is a mixed marriage similar to marriages of different religious, racial, and socioeconomic backgrounds. Yet we heard very few stories of social ostracism by parents or friends, far fewer than we expected to find when we began our research.

We wanted to know how older women/younger men couples managed to cope with their fears. At the beginning of this project we theorized that the couples we interviewed would experience a great deal of internal pressure from their fears. As the interviews with committed couples progressed we kept probing with our questions, always with the same result — there was a low degree of fear, but still the same fears were there: fear of aging, fear of loss, and fear of disapproval.

Most of our interviewed couples were more than willing to talk, both to us and to each other, about what frightened them, but there were some couples who denied that they felt any fear at all. They also refused to be interviewed. Through a third party we heard their reaction to a request for an interview: "There's nothing different about us. We have no problems and nothing to be afraid of. There is really nothing to discuss."

It may be that what these couples say is true. On the other hand, their fears may have been too frightening to face; it may have been impossible for them to admit they had any fears at all. No matter how long you have known them, this kind of couple will never mention, let alone discuss, their age difference. If the topic of older women with younger men comes up, they will ignore it or change the subject. The issue is taboo. They deny its existence.

Psychologically speaking, denial is one possible way to handle a fear. It is not the best way, because in order to deny fear, the individual must cut himself off from his feelings. Fear that is denied will only surface at some later date, probably in some other form.

Unspoken fears are a frequent cause of broken relationships. When people are afraid to discuss their real fears, they will focus on red herrings. Thus, the man who insists that his wife will be an irresponsible mother if she goes to work may really be afraid of losing her to another man. If he never faces his real fear, it will never be resolved. The couple instead puts their energy into an issue that covers up another issue. Misunderstandings will ensue. The fear continues unspoken.

Older women/younger men couples who deny their fears may fight instead over money, the children, or time spent together. This takes the heat off the fear of aging or fear of being left. However, if a real fear is ignored, it may grow larger. It can even be translated into depression or a physical ailment. A couple may go to the extreme of ending the relationship in order to relieve the severe pressure of their un-spoken fears. While denial of fear is an effective way of coping with a short-term situation, it is, in the long run, a potentially explosive element for a relationship.

Acknowledgment of what is frightening to a person is the beginning of the ability to manage anxiety instead of allow-ing unspoken fears to destroy the relationship. Older woman/younger man couples who decide to build a life together are less fearful because they have developed an impressive array of coping devices.

The most widely used method of coping is simple reassur-ance. When we asked twenty-six-year-old Mike Bayer how he handles his fears for the future, he mentioned his fear of Mary's aging. The way Mary looks is important to him, but he believes exterior beauty becomes less important as the relationship goes on.

"I feel as you learn to love someone more, internal beauty becomes more important and it makes the external even more beautiful. Sometimes you meet someone who is not very attractive, almost hard to look at. Then you get to know them and you think that person's attractive. So I think her internal beauty will far exceed her external aging."

As Mike feels closer to Mary, her beauty increases. He accepts the idea that she will age. He expects to continue to find her attractive.

Mary Bayer discusses her own aging process. "I see my life as positive and exciting. I don't know what's ahead, but I have the feeling that it's going to be positively more wonder-ful and I'm going to have something to say about it. I've always thought of myself as living to be really old and always being able to get around and do a lot of things. I see myself as very youthful at thirty-nine. I know that there are certain things that are inevitable and that I will have no control over, that one day I will be eighty. The only thing I can do is stay as physically fit as I can so I can enjoy life. I have good genes; my family is quite healthy."

Mary is self-confident; she is determined to work at staying healthy. She reassures herself about the future and, at the same time, she realistically accepts the aging process.

Time alone helps a couple substitute security for fear. As a woman's trust in her relationship grows over the years, she can let the fears float away. Initially, the woman in the relationship does have more fears, and the younger man needs to do a certain amount of reassuring.

Louise Fletcher, forty-seven, discussed her relationship with twenty-three-year-old Morgan Mason in an interview for the Los Angeles *Times*. "At the beginning," she said, "I was quite uptight about the age thing — much more than he was. He kept saying, 'I'm not like most people of my age. You'll find out. Trust me.' But all I could think was 'Oh my God, what am I going to tell my kids (John, 17; Andrew, 15)?' He told me I'd get over that, and he was right. I have.

"Now I hardly think of the age difference at all. Morgan's so mature for his age. In fact, he's the old fogey in the relationship. If I'd met Morgan earlier, when I was full of fear about almost everything, I'd have dismissed the whole thing out of hand. I'd have never given it a chance. But I'd learned a little by the time we met. I'd decided that what's happening now in life is more important than what may happen in ten years' time. And so I did give it a chance. I still find it hard to realize how young he is. But I try to live for now. Every now and again, of course, I wonder about ten years' time and what will happen. Morgan's unconcerned, but I've been his age and I can think what his priorities may well be by then.

"I wonder if I'll still be working? I know my kids will be grown up and gone, so will I be alone? And is anyone going to care about me then, when I'm not even as attractive as I am now? If I thought too much about it I'd scare myself to death and never come out of the bedroom. So I try not to."[1]

Ms. Fletcher's remarks reflect the experiences of many of those we interviewed. Time and her ability to live in the present helped her overcome her fearfulness. She sets her fears aside in order to live as she wishes. This coping device looks like denial but is actually quite different. In denial, fear is completely ignored. Coping with fear includes acknowledging that fear, deciding to live with it or, perhaps, in spite of it.

Reframing is another way older woman/younger man couples manage potentially threatening situations. Reframing is the ability to take a problem and turn it into an advantage.

For instance, when Paul Stefano, twenty-seven, and his wife, Liz, thirty-seven, come home from parties where other people have reacted strangely to their relationship, they go over the incidents and laugh about them. They become co-conspirators. Thus, they are more intimately joined together and not wedged apart by the experience.

Susan Howard sees Peter Levin's charm with women as a validation of her good taste. How easy it might be to feel threatened. "When I met Peter I became aware of the fact that he went like a little hummingbird to every woman in the place and sipped and tasted. I thought it was the most fascinating thing I'd ever seen. I was very taken by it because it wasn't a come-on. He wasn't pushing anybody; he was just there. I thought to myself, 'This man really likes women.' And that's good."

Susan could feel jealous when Peter "goes humming."

Instead she notices his enjoyment of women and feels pleased that other women appreciate him the same way she does.

Another way of coping with fear is to use our adult reasoning capacities. Often we heard couples say that there is no guaranteed security in life or in marriage. In our time, divorce is common; a husband or wife may leave the relationship at any time and for any reason. For an older woman considering a relationship with a younger man to say to herself, "He may leave you later," is almost beside the point.

A thirty-eight-year-old woman living with a twenty-three-year-old man told us, "I was afraid of growing old and looking older before he does and the relationship ending because of that, but I guess I've been in enough relationships that ended anyway, so that's not really a very good argument."

While it is true that older women are not generally valued by our society, it is not true that no one values older women. Clearly some men prefer older women. Such men can be devoted, loyal husbands. There is no reason to assume a young man will leave an older woman for a younger woman. If he leaves, it may well be for the usual reasons, the reasons that can end any relationship: lack of communication, unresolved conflicts, or incompatible value systems. Several women told us they thought it would be more likely for their man to leave them for another older woman than a younger woman, since these men are usually attracted to older women. For example, when Jennie Churchill was fifty-five she was divorced from her husband of fifteen years, thirty-six-year-old George Cornwallis-West. Shortly thereafter, Cornwallis-West married an actress, Mrs. Pat Campbell, who was only a few years younger than Lady Churchill.

A twenty-five-year-old writer living with a woman who is twenty-three years older than he discussed the aging issue.

"I see the question of her aging differently than most people. She is forty-eight years old. She is in excellent health. She has never been a typically pretty woman, but at this age she is handsome. For the next ten or fifteen years she'll look much the same as now. As I see it, the problem is that over the next ten or fifteen years, she will watch me age. How will she feel as she watches me, her young lover, becoming a balding, pot-bellied, fortyish man?"

This young man points out a truth that is usually overlooked in all the worry about the woman's aging. Some young men age noticeably early in life. Logically, the young man has as much reason to worry as the older woman. Of course, there are other reasons why the aging of women gets more attention than the aging of men and why some women are terrified of growing older with younger men. In most societies, the value of an aging woman is far less than the value of an older man. Because of this double standard a woman is naturally far more concerned about her aging process than a man is about his.

Another reason the people we've interviewed don't worry too much about the future is because they have developed new value systems in which there is a high priority on living fully in the present without being overly concerned about the future. Throughout the interviews we've heard statements like "We could be dead in fifteen years, why worry about it," "Our life together is wonderful; if it is not wonderful in twenty years we will deal with it at that time," "He has given me three happy years; if he goes tomorrow I will not regret this experience." Two uncommon values stand out in these remarks. The first is a desire to live in the present, one day at a time. The second is a lessening of the need for security.

People who live in the present consciously choose to stop

worrying about what may happen later. They accept the fact that danger is out there and reason this way: "If I can do something to avoid an unhappy event in the future I will do it. If there is nothing I can do, then I will let go of the worry. Worrying unnecessarily does not solve a problem; it only aggravates it."

The more time a couple spends on pursuing goals, the less time there is to spend on worrying about aging or breaking up. The goals may be as simple as enjoying a relaxed day picnicking or as future-oriented as building a career. Living in the present means feeling the warmth of the sun, the smells of the trees and grass on a picnic, instead of thinking about yesterday's mistakes or tomorrow's work. It means appreciating each step along the way to the career goal. It is an attitude that aims at increasing pleasure in life.

The illusory security many people seek puts the focus on the future. In part, the need for security is based on the belief that couples should stay together forever. This assumption leads to the need for a guarantee that the relationship will last forever. It is no small accomplishment to reduce the hold of this belief.

A lessening need for security comes from self-confidence and experience in life. Many of the older women we've interviewed appear to have both. Women who have once made a life of their own have the inner knowledge they can do it again if need be. Mature women know that there are no guarantees. Any commitment can be withdrawn. Liz Stefano speaks for many of our interviewees: "When I feel afraid about our relationship ending, I remind myself that whatever happens, I can handle it. I have made it through separation, divorce, graduate school, establishing a practice, love affairs, and loss of parents. Life with Paul is delightful. Life alone would also be delightful, but it would be different in many ways. I was content when I was single. I'm certain I can do it again. I want this relationship to last, but I want it to last in a quality way.

"I ended my first marriage because I wanted to change myself and my life-style. My first husband and I were the perfect couple — in everyone else's eyes. My brother-in-law and sister-in-law had a mess of a life together, fights, economic problems, constant chaos. Everyone thought they'd break up. It doesn't make sense that they're still together and we broke up. I've learned that life doesn't always make sense. Life is definitely not fair. We do not always get what we want. And there are simply no guarantees in regard to staying together."

Liz knows some realities of life. She has struggled and survived. Because she believes in herself, the loss of a husband, for whatever reason, would not ruin her life. This understanding enables her to risk marriage to a younger man. It helps her cope with her fears about the future.

Overall, it is probably the level of self-confidence of each of the people involved in an older woman/younger man relationship that will determine whether that relationship succeeds or fails. In the case of the woman, the more secure she is as an individual, the less she is bothered by the thought of being left. In part, the feared loss of a mate is based on the fact that often a woman does not make her own living. Only a tiny percentage of our woman interviewees were financially dependent on their men. Most have thriving careers. If the relationship ended, the woman could take care of her own material needs with very little change.

The other major loss would be the loss of emotional support. Again, most of these women have plentiful resources. Like Liz, they have experienced separation, divorce, and ended love affairs. They have strong support from friends and relatives. More important, they know how to use this support to get them through a loss. They are confident about their ability to meet that possibility.

A forty-eight-year-old artist says of her relationship with a thirty-one-year-old man: "Somehow the idea that this relationship could come to an end is not as terrifying to me as it would have been ten years ago. I make my own living, such as it is; I'm comfortable. I never want to be economically or socially dependent on a man again. That way, if either one of us should ever want to leave, my way of life would not be seriously affected. I would nurse my broken heart and go on with my life."

Most of the women we interviewed are unusual people. They have a strong sense of identity, which surfaces in the way they talk, the way they groom themselves, and the way they carry their bodies. Quite a few look younger than their age, but not because they don't have signs of aging. They look younger because they are vital people.

Their confidence extends into the future. A thirty-five-year-old professor put it this way: "I'm going to be one of these Auntie Mame types, zipping around, hopefully being very vital and interesting and doing things up until ninety or a hundred."

The men we interviewed also feel basically confident. At the same time that he is busy expressing his fears for the future, Peter Levin, thirty-one, is coming up with a variety of ways to cope with those fears: "About fears relating to differences in physical pacing and keeping up:

"One, if she's slower or weaker it's a natural situation for stroking those traditional male parts of me that say, 'He should protect the woman, do the heavy work, etcetera.' My belief in the women's liberation movement notwithstanding, I still enjoy chivalry.

"Two, since entering this older woman/younger man relationship I feel I've been able to admit more readily those times that I'm drained and exhausted. Perhaps because of this, I will not physically burn myself out and die earlier than her, as so many men do in the name of malehood, the 'stronger of the sexes.'

"Three, if a discrepancy does occur in our physical energy levels, our relationship, as I think is typical of many older woman/younger man relationships, offers maximum freedom and sense of individuality in helping deal with the discrepancy. I can go off and do things alone with my additional energy and not threaten our relationship. So can she! It seems to me that the expectation of same-age couples that each will always have the same energy level, all the time, works against a 'freedom to be' way of relating.

"If she gets physically sick:

"One, I welcome the chance to exercise the nurturing part of myself.

"Two, I will feel cheated if it's a permanent, debilitating thing — same as I would feel with a same-age wife. That's the point: I don't feel older women have any more of a chance of extreme debilitation than same-age women. Susan takes good care of herself. I believe 'old people' does not have to mean 'sick people' — it's a myth.

"My fears about my relationship with Susan:

"One, she will get bored with me because she is even more capable than I am of making life exciting for herself and not getting trapped.

"Two, she will not have patience to watch me still do my 'growing' and 'experiencing' of things in life which she may already have experienced. (Irony: I often feel that way about women who are my age.)

"My feelings about relationships with women my age: She is not grown yet; she needs to experience more of life, as do I. But with a same-age woman I feel that I have to carry the burden of keeping her channels open (as well as my own), I have to make sure that she takes care of her own life and keeps on growing. My feelings with Susan: Susan has no misconceptions about what she is getting into. She has lived and will continue to operate in such a way as to not become trapped. She will work against all the goblins that attack relationships — boredom, routine, sameness, etcetera — and will carry her share of the load in doing this.

"In general: Most fears about our relationship are the same ones I would have in any relationship: Will she get bored with me? Will I get bored with her? Will one of us be disabled in a car accident? Will I get cancer and take five pitiful years to die? Will she? Will I take up tennis while she doesn't? Will she take up tennis while I get fat watching sports on TV? Will I get fat? Will she? What does the future hold? Will I be different? Will she be different? Is the love we have now too fleeting an experience on which to base a lifetime commitment? In relationships with same-age women I frequently have had fears that they were not ready yet for a serious commitment, even when they said they were. Myself, on the other hand, I always trusted. Well, sometimes doubts crept in — Am I fooling myself? Can I be *that* sure I'll feel this way forever? Can anyone tell how he/she will feel in the future?"

Peter handles his fears well because, first of all, he is willing to admit they are there. Then he proceeds to use most of the positive techniques described in this chapter.

(1) Reassurance — he reminds himself of the advantages of his life with Susan.

(2) Reframing — he looks at negative events in a positive way, such as seeing illness as an opportunity to be nurturing.

(3) Use of reason — since he and Susan share responsibilities in this relationship, he thinks he may live in a less pressured way, thus extending his life. The flexibility of their relationship allows them to adapt to unexpected future events.

(4) Setting different value priorities — Peter stresses sharing responsibilities, communication, independence.

(5) Self-confidence — Peter has faith in his ability to manage problems. He also believes in Susan's skills for making her life and their relationship work well.

Management of fear does not mean that fear ceases to exist. A fear will return from time to time and will have to be handled again, for in addition to personal fears, older woman / younger man couples must deal with the fear of breaking accepted social rules. It is natural to be frightened when deliberately ignoring many of society's conventions. There is a possibility of being punished for daring to do things differently. What conventions are these couples ignoring? What taboos may they be consciously or unconsciously violating?

5 ·

BREAKING RULES

WE HAVE SEEN THAT OLDER WOMAN/YOUNGER MAN couples face a great deal of external pressure in the form of disapproval by family, friends, and even strangers. They also have to deal with severe internal pressures expressed as fear, guilt, and anxiety. Why is the reaction, both from without and within, so intense? What are they doing that is wrong? Such a powerful reaction comes from a powerful source: essentially, these couples have broken too many social rules. It is both the importance of these rules and the number of rules broken that cause the strong reactions.

All societies have prohibitions which range from very important taboos to less severe cultural conventions.

Taboos form unwritten codes restricting certain human types of behaviors: they are prohibitions against thinking, saying, or doing a particular act, enforced through threat of punishment. The purpose of taboos is to protect society from any danger to the continued survival of the family, the tribe, or the nation. Taboos guard the chief acts of life, such as birth, coming to puberty, marriage, and sexual functions. By keeping atypical behavior on a small scale, taboos maintain social order, and thereby ensure the continuation of society itself.

Taboos are a powerful force for social order only because their consequences are dreaded. Families, friends, the law, religion, and cultural myths in the form of literature, television, theater, and movies all remind us what will happen if important taboos are broken. The message from these sources says, "If you break the taboo, doom is inevitable." In other words, people who break taboos will be punished.

In his book *Totem and Taboo*, Freud says that "taboos concern actions for which there is a strong desire. . . . For what nobody desires to do does not have to be forbidden, and certainly whatever is expressly forbidden must be an object of desire. . . . The original pleasure to do the forbidden still continues . . . there exists an unconscious wish to transgress."[1] However, the fear of transgressing is intense. Ordinarily, it is greater than the desire to transgress the taboo.

Older women with younger men have overcome the fear of transgressing taboos and have, as a result, become taboo themselves. Why is this so? Freud has an explanation that makes sense. He says taboo-breaking people are a threat because, by their example, they tempt others to violate the taboo. The presence of the older woman/younger man taboo couple brings up in other people powerfully ambivalent feelings. One of those feelings is envy; another is anger. Why should this couple be allowed what is forbidden to others? The result is an intense negative emotional response to older women/younger men couples.

During the time when we were doing our research on these couples, we discovered we were dealing with a genuinely taboo situation. Not only was the behavior of these couples treated as a taboo, but as a subject of conversation the topic was often discussable solely as a generalization, almost never as a familiar experience.

We were amazed to see how many people forgot to tell us about friends and relatives who were older woman/younger man couples. We would mention the topic of this book to someone. They would respond, "Great! How interesting." Then two weeks later, six months later, they'd say, "You know what, my mother is ten years older than my father." Or "Aunt Tillie is older than Uncle Bob. I forgot to tell you. It was a kind of family secret. No one ever discussed it. I got the feeling we weren't supposed to know." We kept stumbling over secret older woman/younger man relationships.

Two sisters told us about a favorite aunt of theirs who had married a man three years younger than she. Their aunt was so concerned about anyone finding out about the age difference that she had every legal document she could lay her hands on changed to make her two years younger than her husband. The years went by and in the course of time, her husband passed away. The matter seemed to be forgotten.

When the aunt reached the age of sixty-two she applied for Social Security benefits. As one of the sisters told us, "Aunt Barb had covered her tracks so well, that when the time came to present the documents with proof of age, not one could be found that did not give her age as fifty-seven."

We were intrigued by the number of times we heard variations of this story. Gradually we began to get the idea that there were probably many more relationships in which the woman was older than the man than most people were willing to admit. In addition, family members have a very peculiar style of communicating this information both to each other and to outsiders. We have discovered that countless older woman/younger man relationships exist, but that family members have an unconscious agreement not to talk about it openly among themselves.

Most of the people we have talked to were raised in families that treated these relationships as skeletons in the closets, not so well hidden, perhaps, as illegitimacy or imprisonment, but still not to be discussed in polite company. The children in the family got the idea early. Aune Jane is older than Uncle Ernest. Not quite nice, something wrong there, don't ask questions and, above all, make sure that it doesn't happen to you! The message is clear and strong. After this kind of training, it is not surprising that people forget the obvious.

All societies have some rules that are unmentionable. These rules are in operation all around us, but not on a conscious level. For example, it is taboo to touch our genitals in public. If someone is doing so, we don't say to ourselves, "He is breaking the touching rule." Instead we react with automatic disgust or rejection. It is a rule we are not consciously aware of. And if we are aware of the rule, we probably would not discuss it. It is against the rules of society to talk openly of certain topics.

Another example of the unmentionable taboo might be the rules surrounding elimination. Everybody does it, everybody knows that everybody does it, but nobody talks about it and it is done only in private. Elimination is an essential everyday occurrence, yet a public announcement of that fact would produce a reaction of disgust, thus reinforcing the subject as secret and unmentionable.

Attempts to bring unmentionable rules or taboos into the open may not succeed. British psychiatrist R. D. Laing points out the following behavioral response to a discussion of unmentionable rules. First the person will feel confused; then he or she will resist accepting the information. Almost immediately, the ideas that the person has just heard will be denied or forgotten.

Anyone trying to read or even write about unmentionable rules will have the same reaction. Confusion, resistance, and denial collude to form an effective barrier to an investigation of the taboo issue.

In this chapter we have broken a societal rule that says *some rules are unmentionable*. We have also broken the rule that says *we must forget that some rules are unmentionable*. The second rule erases the knowledge of the first rule. But by discussing the rules about older woman/younger man relationships in bold print, we are forcing those rules to a conscious level.

The process goes something like this:

(1) Older women and younger men must not mate. (The unmentionable rule).

(2) We are not consciously aware that the rule above exists and we are not consciously aware of the reasons behind it. (The rule is forgotten.)

(3) Then, when confronted with the reality of an older woman/younger man relationship, we simply have a thought or feeling like "This is wrong," "I'm too afraid to do it," "It can't possibly last," or "How can he love an old woman?"

Now that we know how an unmentionable taboo functions, what are the real reasons behind the perception of the older woman/younger man relationship as taboo?

The first reason is the incest taboo, the strongest taboo in our culture. While older women/younger men are not committing incest, the age difference between them reminds people of the forbidden sexual relationship between mothers and sons. Very strong feelings of social disapproval arise about this taboo because of its extreme cultural, historical, and psychological significance. The incest taboo, in part, developed in order to maintain family harmony. If, for example, a mother mated with her son, the family system would break down. Father and son would be in competition for the same mate, thus producing dangerous levels of jealousy and discord.

The incest taboo protects the child's development by fostering sexual and social separation from the family. The child is encouraged to go outside the family to meet sexual stimulation needs.

This taboo may have developed to assist the economic development of society, since marrying into other groups multiplied the resources of each group. In addition, the issue of inheritance would be endlessly confused without the incest taboo. If father and son were allowed to breed with the same woman, it would be impossible to sort out lines of heritage.

Furthermore, society has long since learned that incest is genetically unsound. Physical and mental deficiencies occur much more frequently when family members interbreed.

Today the incest taboo is still in full force, but there has been a noticeable change in its operation. Incest used to be unmentionable. The secrecy rule is lifting, so that incest is now discussed in books, on film and television.

This taboo still operates to influence the response of people to the older woman/younger man couple. If the woman looks older than the man the response of the observer may be "What's he doing with her? She looks old enough to be his mother."

Compounding the effects of the incest taboo is the impact in our society of Freud's theory of the Oedipus complex. Even though psychoanalytic thought has been greatly modified over the last seventy years, there has been a popularization of the early theory that "looking for a mother" is neurotic — that is, sick, abnormal. In our chapter called "Who's Looking for a Mother?" we examine this belief.

Although taboos are the most fearsome rules that cultures impose on their members, there are other significant social rules that, while they are not quite taboos, still have immense impact. Older women/younger men couples break two of those important rules that are connected to the survival of a society. To survive, a society must continue to produce people. Therefore, the rule exists that couples should produce children, a powerful cultural convention. The second significant rule, embedded in the teachings of some branches of Christianity, is that sex is acceptable only for procreation.

The profound negative emotional reaction to couples who don't want children is proof of the severity of this rule. Since older women and younger men couples only rarely decide to produce children, these couples are perceived as a threat to the perpetuation of the species, for several reasons. Throughout history, societies have needed to replace populations depleted by war, famine, or disease. For this and other reasons, the greatest joy in family life has been the birth of a child. The child is the society's future; the child is the major reason for the existence of the family; the child is immortality for the parents. One need only call to mind that in our society one of the greatest tragedies is the barren couple. (Consider the word *barren*; it conjures up the vision of a wasteland.)

Countering the deep emotional, biological urge toward reproduction are recent accelerated social changes, such as fear of overpopulation, greater numbers of working women, and the movement toward more personal freedom for women. Because of these trends, many more couples are having few or no children. But the age-old conditioning for species survival is still powerful enough to cause deep conflict in the individuals who decide not to have children, and in other people's attitudes toward them.

Even today the friends of a childless couple are reluctant to ask why the couple has no children. If it were truly acceptable to be childless, then the topic would not be so sensitive. The couple would be able to laugh off pressure from the potential grandparents. But even today, we still need discussion groups and therapy to help people make the guilt-ridden decision whether or not to have children.

Only two of the fifty couples we interviewed had a child of their own. Two pairs planned to have a child later. For a variety of reasons, all the other couples had decided not to have children. About ten percent of the women we interviewed intend never to have children. At least half of the younger men do not plan to have children. The other half either already have children from a previous marriage or are helping to raise the older woman's children. On the whole, older women/younger men couples do not produce children and, consequently, break a major societal rule.

Since such couples do not usually produce children, it is assumed that their sexual activity must be for pleasure alone. This brings up the second major rule those couples break. Sexual pleasure for its own sake is not universally sanctioned in our society. Over and over, as we told people about this book, they would respond as though we had made some sort of sexual innuendo. One man told us that the proposed title of our book, *Older Women/Younger Men*, was sexy. What, we wondered, is sexy about the title? There were leers and suggestive jokes often enough for us to get the idea that most people assume that older women/younger men relationships exist primarily for erotic pleasure.

And if it is true that older women and younger men are a good sexual match, then it may also be true, as Francine du Plessix Gray wrote in a recent article in *The New York Times*, "In any society tainted by puritanism . . . such a relationship is bound to remain taboo simply because it is too much fun. . . ."[2]

The rules that *marriages should produce children* and that *sex is acceptable only for procreation* are powerful cultural conventions. They are so strong that they are close to the taboo level. However, the violation of cultural rules or conventions of behavior is less severely punished than taboos. If a cultural rule is broken, the worst possible consequence would be withdrawal of social acceptance.

Cultural rules, unlike taboos, are conscious. We know they exist; we know what they are. They help preserve an accepted way of perceiving and doing things. "Respectable" people follow traditional cultural rules. They wear clothes appropriate to the occasion. They make the proper remarks at dinner parties, weddings, and funerals. They marry the correct partners. Older women/younger men couples break a series of important cultural rules. These deviations are more easily forgiven than broken taboos, but still, when added up, they combine to make an older woman/younger man relationship a troublesome business.

There are endless cultural rules seemingly ignored by the older woman/younger man couple. The idea that *men must dominate women* is one example, with a long history in Western culture. We have come to believe that a man should be reinforced in his concept of his own superiority. According to social custom, a man may marry down but women should marry up. This practice helps assure male dominance. Despite the challenge of the seventies, the appropriateness of male dominance is a widely held belief.

Observers of older women/younger men couples expect the older women to dominate the younger men, by virtue of age and experience. However, the issue of dominance as experienced by the couples we interviewed is different from the expectation. Dominance is such an important issue that we have devoted a chapter to exploring its meaning for the older woman/younger man couple. For the moment, we will say that nearly all committed couples of this type break the rule that says men must dominate women.

There is a rule that says that *members of a society should conform to its rules*. The older women/younger men couples we interviewed are usually nonconformists. Even though a free society ostensibly protects nonconformists, the major thrust of our society is to conform. Powerful forces collude to enforce our system of rules. The rules are backed by religion, education, politics, the law, families, and the communications media. People who do not conform to the rules of our culture, whether they are sensible rules or not, are considered sick, stupid, crazy, or criminal. People therefore assume that older women and younger men who form permanent relationships are deviant members of society and must be treated accordingly.

When a young man falls in love with an older woman, people around him wonder why. He is breaking our cultural rule of *worshiping youth*. Unlike Eastern peoples who respect and honor the old, Americans, in particular, adulate all that is young: young bodies, young faces, young ideas, and, especially, young women.

In Western cultures, aging women are almost totally devalued. In her sixth *Diary*, Anaïs Nin says, ". . . We do not forgive a woman aging. . . . The slightest wilting is tragic in women because we make it so . . . her aging does not constitute a new kind of beauty, hierarchic, gothic, classical."[3] We see that anger is generated toward older women and younger men for ignoring the custom of youth worship. We wonder if the interest of younger men in older women heralds a change in this cultural rule.

In most societies *young men are reserved for young women*. In primitive times this rule could have had great importance to the survival of a tribe. If too many young men mated with older women the tribe could die off from the lack of repopulation. Such liaisons could also have triggered competition and jealousy between older men and younger men for mates. We were surprised at the degree of anger that accompanied the criticism of older women who "took partners away from younger women."

When Susan Howard, forty-six, and Peter Levin, thirty-one, first started seeing each other, Susan was in group therapy. A young woman in her group was indignant about Susan's affair with Peter. She told Susan that Susan had already had her chance in life and had no business taking Peter out of circulation when there were young women around who might want him. The young woman had no particular interest in Peter but was outraged by Susan's apparent insensitivity to the basic issue of fair competition for mates. Susan believes that this primitive anger would not have come out if it hadn't been for the group therapy situation, where it is permissible to say what you really think and feel.

Thirty-five-year-old Jim took forty-five-year-old Janis to a family get-together very early in their relationship. Jim's aunt questioned Janis about the problems in Janis's relationship with a younger man, and finally concluded the conversation with this zinger: "If women like you keep taking the younger men, how's my daughter ever going to find anybody?" The aunt was reiterating the cultural rule that young men are reserved for young women.

As we see, older women/younger men couples break both taboos and cultural rules. Their relationship reminds people of the incest taboo, the rule against not producing children, and the rule that sex is only for procreation. In addition, these couples are rejecting certain cherished cultural beliefs, such as that young men must be reserved for young women, that youth, not age, is valuable, that conforming is important, and that men have to dominate women. Considering the accumulation of taboos and cultural rules that older women/younger men relationships break, it is not surprising that the idea of forming such an alliance would be extremely frightening to most people.

As long as there are taboos and cultural rules, society must have ways to enforce them. Enforcement is most often accomplished through punishment. If people choose a socially unacceptable behavior, a violation of taboo or tradition, consequences must follow or social order will disintegrate. Older women/younger men couples can be punished from within by continual self-imposed anxiety about their relationship and on the outside by social disapproval manifested as criticism, anger, or ostracism. Anyone who chooses an older woman or a younger man for a life partner can expect some stress from both sources or at least one of them.

If we break rules, our culture teaches us what the consequences will be. Many films about older women and younger men end tragically. The older woman sometimes looks like an aging fool clinging to a reluctant younger man as in *Sweet Bird of Youth*. Often she leaves him for his own good, as in *Tea and Sympathy* or *Anatomy of a Seduction*. Over and over these stories reinforce the idea that "doom is inevitable." The dialogue is filled with classic warnings like "It can't last," "He'll leave you," "You'll look old," and "What about ten years from now?"

According to traditional thinking, the only time an older woman and a younger man can seriously consider being together is if the woman is going to die. In a recent film called *Love, Pain and the Whole Damn Thing*, college dropout Timothy Bottoms meets mid-thirties spinster Maggie Smith on a European jaunt. They take an intense dislike to each other on sight. Later, they fall in love. He is looking for some meaning in life; she is trying to find some meaning in her impending death.

Love, Pain, and the Whole Damn Thing is a beautiful movie about people growing up, growing older and facing up to the really frightening things in life, like death. In the end the young man commits himself to marriage with a dying woman. We believe that the couple is actually allowed to marry, rather than just live together until Maggie Smith dies, only because the heroine is, in fact, as good as dead. Message: an older woman can fall in love with and marry a younger man only if one of them dies shortly thereafter, preferably the woman. What is a common plot in movies and books is not necessarily common in life.

Even though there are countless numbers of older woman/younger man romances and marriages, the fantasy persists that the lovers must be parted by malignant forces in the fullest bloom of life. Being torn apart in the midst of their love is possibly their rightful punishment for transgressing the taboos. With this concept as a model of the meaningful older woman/younger man relationship, it is not surprising that the average woman would rather keep her ideas about a relationship with a younger man in the fantasy stage.

In 1978 two major films were made which attempted to tell an older woman/younger man story without doom. Both *Moment by Moment* and *Players* were unconvincing, embarrassingly bad movies, perhaps for all the usual reasons — poor writing, direction, and so on — or perhaps underneath all the mistakes was the taboo, the taboo which says, you can tell this story only if it ends tragically. It is important not to underestimate the power of traditional attitudes. Besides the Oedipus story, another of the earliest Greek myths set the model for the older woman/younger man story. Phaedra shamefully falls in love with Hippolitus, her husband's virtuous son by a former marriage. She is determined to have him; he resists; she persists. The story ends with Phaedra's disgrace and the death of the young man.

If no one else punishes an older woman/younger man couple, the couple may punish themselves. Taboos are incorporated within us all. *The taboo feelings are deep within, not at a conscious level.* We repeat, the reasons for the taboo and even the taboo itself may be forgotten. Taboo is internalized as fear or guilt. We found that women suffered more than men from guilt and fear; they spoke of it more often. The messages from inside them were "I'm bad," "This is crazy," "I'm irresponsible." The fear messages in the younger men were "She'll be ashamed of me," "She'll dominate me," "I won't be able to keep her interest."

It is important to see that these messages from the inner self are largely irrational. There is no reason for a woman of forty to believe she is crazy for wanting to marry a twenty-five-year-old man, nor he for wanting to marry her. They are both adults, capable of deciding with whom to spend their lives. The fear messages are internalizations of the taboos and rules, self-punishment for even considering breaking society's rules.

The degree of internal or external punishment depends upon several factors. For instance, the greater the age difference, the stronger the reaction of others will be. The greater the open defiance by the couple, the more far-reaching the negative consequences are likely to be. However, the greater the self-confidence and individuality of the couple, the less the consequences will tend to affect them, even in the face of strong public disapproval.

For instance, in 1977, twenty-one-year-old Mark Goodman married seventy-seven-year-old Ray Goodman. Their marriage made them international celebrities, even though public reaction generally consisted of shock, disgust, and outrage. Contrast that response with the public response to marriages in which the man is far older than the woman. In the cases of Charlie Chaplin, Pablo Picasso, Dr. Benjamin Spock, and Justice William O. Douglas, the responses ranged from surprise to shock. But the women they married are considered fortunate to be able to enjoy the last years of the life of an experienced, creative man. Does anyone think twenty-one-year-old Mark Goodman is fortunate to be able to share the last years of seventy-seven-year-old Ray Goodman's life? A large age difference with the women older is extremely taboo.

The public reaction is strong. But in spite of the negative response, Mark and Ray Goodman seem able to cope. Perhaps their enormous confidence in their love for each other and their tremendous enjoyment of their own celebrity will allow them to survive social outrage.

Open defiance of social rules usually brings severe punishment. Society will tolerate a lot of rule breaking if the persons involved are discreet or at least contrite afterward. In 1969, a thirty-two-year-old Frenchwoman committed suicide as she was about to face the reopening of her trial for having "deviated" a younger man.

At thirty Gabrielle Russier began an affair with a sixteen-year-old student. In spite of a liberal attitude toward sexual matters, the French reacted severely to this "love affair" crime. The usual punishment for the seduction of a minor by a teacher is to fire the teacher. In France, if it can be proved that a female minor gave consent, the charges will be dropped. However, a male minor's consent is ignored.

Gabrielle Russier went through a long, highly publicized trial, was convicted, and then spent several months in jail. She was severely depressed after her release. Then came the news of a new appeal for conviction, a very unusual move, which threatened to open the case again. It appears that she was hounded unmercifully both by the parents of the young man and by the law.

Gabrielle Russier's defenders wondered why she was given such harsh treatment. We believe she broke too many societal rules. She had sex with a minor, who was also her student. She insisted they were in love. She conducted the affair openly, defiantly. She refused to admit she had made a mistake. In the end she was excessively naive and self-destructive. If Mlle. Russier had behaved differently, she would probably have never gone on trial, let alone been imprisoned. Society is cruel to those who break rules without any attempt at discretion or contrition. Her insistence that she would not give up her young lover helped to create the persecution that made her a tragic figure, a modern Phaedra. Her open defiance had to be punished. What society did not do she did to herself.

The Goodmans have broken taboos and cultural rules, but the severest consequence of their marriage is a degree of notoriety. Gabrielle Russier suffered the ultimate consequence for her open love affair with a very young man, harassment to the point of taking her own life. Generally, however, the consequences that the average older woman/younger man couple can expect might be the loss of a friendship, confused or critical reactions from outsiders, or a periodic fear that the relationship can't last.

While older woman/younger man couples have definite problems to deal with, there is no scientific justification for a prediction of doom. The "doom" myth is a function of taboo, keeping individuals in line through fear, keeping the numbers of older woman/younger man couples to a minimum. Its purpose is to maintain social order. As one woman put it, "What if all the young men were taken by older women?" What indeed!

6 ·

POWER AND DOMINANCE

THE YOUNG COUPLE SITTING OPPOSITE THE THERAPIST were obviously uncomfortable, so the therapist came to the point quickly. "You told me over the phone that you thought you needed a marriage counselor. What kind of problems are you having?" The young woman looked anxiously at her husband and said, "Do you want to tell her or shall I?" The young man shrugged his shoulders and replied, "Maybe you better tell her. After all, I'm not the one who's worried about it; you are." The wife braced herself and blurted out, "Well, you see, I'm twenty-seven years old and my husband is twenty-two. We've been married for a year and we get along just fine. But I have always wondered if marrying a man five years younger than me meant there was something wrong with me. I've been so bothered by this idea that I asked my husband if he would go to a marriage counselor with me. He doesn't understand why I'm so upset about this and, frankly, neither do I. But I am, and here we are!"

She sat back and drew a long breath. Her husband reached out and took her hand. The therapist regarded them for a moment and then said to the wife, "Why do you think there's something wrong with you?" "Well," the young woman said, "I am really worried about being a dominating female. I don't like that idea of myself. I am kind of strong and independent. Besides that, I have a job in which I supervise a lot of people and I make more money than my husband does. I guess I'm thinking that if I'm a strong person and I married a younger man, maybe I am a dominating woman and I don't want to be one."

The therapist looked inquiringly at the husband. "Do you feel that your wife dominates you?" "Not at all," said the husband; "I can't figure out where she got that idea. We get along just fine." The therapist turned back to the wife. "Where did you get that idea?" The young woman frowned and then explained, "I kind of see it this way. Men are supposed to dominate women. They're supposed to be older and make more money. I don't really like the idea of anyone dominating me; as a matter of fact, I probably wouldn't put up with it for a minute. But I can't get the idea out of my head that there must be something wrong with me for marrying a man who is younger than me and whose salary isn't as big."

In most cultures it is taken for granted that men must dominate, at least overtly. And it is generally assumed that in a relationship where a woman is older than a man, the woman is dominant. That, of course, won't do because men are supposed to be dominant at all times. Manhood is equated with dominance and femininity with submission. These concepts are so deeply ingrained in our cultural thinking that a healthy young woman in a happy marriage has to visit a marriage counselor to allay her fears!

Essentially, a person who dominates is one who is attempting to control the actions of another person. The person who takes control does so by virtue of some kind of power. That power may have a physical, mental, or emotional form, such as more muscles, more money, or just a greater ability to manipulate others. The person who controls, or dominates, another by using one or more of those powers is often perceived as innately superior, while the one without those powers is seen as inferior. This concept raises some basic questions about power in male-female relationships.

Tina Carey is forty-seven years old and a top executive with a well-known business firm. She is a person of rare charm, extremely attractive physically, taller than average, willowy, graceful, and composed. She has been married twice. For the past two years she has been involved in a relationship with a man eleven years her junior. We asked her what she thought about women being older than men in committed, long-term relationships.

Tina smiled and then she chuckled. She tilted her chair back and shifted her long legs to the top of her desk, ankles neatly crossed. She made a church steeple with her fingers and peered into them for a moment. Finally she said, "I was brought up in a very conventional way. My family is quite traditional. I guess I grew up believing that when I married, my husband should be older than I, smarter, of course, richer, I hoped, and although I would have a career, he would probably be more successful than I was. And, needless to say," and here she glanced at the length of herself and chuckled again, "he should be taller than I am. Well, I've lived a little longer now and a number of preconceptions about life and relationships have changed. I really don't think that it is necessary or even advisable for a man to be older, richer, or wiser than his wife. However," she said, "there's one hang-up I haven't gotten past. I still prefer my man to be taller than I am. There's really no legitimate reason that I should feel this way, but I do, and I don't think I'm going to make any attempt to change it."

In most societies male dominance over the female is an accepted cultural convention. It is not a truth. Nothing brings that fact home more clearly than the parade of powerless husbands who pass through the family therapist's office. To complicate matters, it is also conventional to believe that in a marriage, one person must dominate. How do we derive the idea that one person must dominate? Part of the issue has to do with sociological norms and part has to do with drawing conclusions about the basic behavior of human beings.

We learn by observation about the conventions of power and dominance. A person looks at the world around him or her, perceives certain patterns of behavior and draws the conclusion that this is how things are done. Hierarchy of command is a major observable pattern in our society. There is only one captain to a ship, one person who makes the significant decisions, one person who is ultimately in charge.

In addition, we live in a patriarchal system, a system in which the male is given more power than the female. Power, in our society, is derived from age, wealth, level of education, outstanding personal achievement, and, sometimes, just being bigger than the next guy. Since statistically the man has more of all of these attributes, we assume that the husband must have the dominant role. The male assumes his right to dominate by equating dominance with power. Besides that, there is the idea that if power is not utilized, a vacuum is created. Most people believe that if the male does not firmly dominate the relationship, the female will move into this vacuum.

In this way, the status quo is accepted as a given truth and the person then proceeds to translate these observations into guidelines for his or her own life. From generation to generation, the guideline is that men must be older, richer, wiser, or bigger than their wives or they will not dominate. If the male is not dominant, the relationship is out of balance. Things are not as they should be.

Even in families where the official guidelines about relationships are not particularly rigid, outside pressure is brought to bear until the person's thinking conforms to the norm. During one of our interviews a woman told us that she came from a large family in which an unusual number of female relatives were married to men who were younger than they. The age differences were not really significant, a few years or a few months, but the family joked about it a lot among themselves. The woman told us, "When I was a child I didn't think that wives' being older than their husbands was even unusual, but as I grew older I found out from friends that this was a rather odd situation. I guess my family was just abnormal."

We found it interesting that this woman concluded that wives' being older than husbands was ultimately abnormal. She became convinced that what could be seen as merely unusual or different was deviant. Since deviance from the norm is usually defined as sick, bad, or crazy, the connotation is negative.

Cultures constantly reinforce the idea that men must dominate, even in a day and age when many women are breaking down conventional sex-role concepts by working with men on almost every occupational level. Even when husband and wife are professional equals, the concept of male dominance in a relationship is still subtly reinforced.

A recent "Newsmaker" article in the Los Angeles *Times* discussed a married couple who are both doctors. At the age of thirty-seven, each one heads an emergency room unit at a hospital. The article concludes with this comment: "And although each doctor is the boss at work, they know who is head honcho when the rubber gloves are off. 'Fred told me I can be the boss at home and he is the boss on the boat. It works out fine,' Dr. Karen said."[1]

The division of labor, as usual, is that the lady doctor is

responsible for the home. Dr. Fred, of course, is the boss of the boat. But, most important, Dr. Fred is the one who decides who plays which role. Even with all things being equal — their ages, their achievements, their incomes — Dr. Fred is the ultimate authority who determines who fulfills what role outside the emergency room. We repeat Dr. Karen's words, "Fred told me I can be . . ." Once the white coats and stethoscopes are discarded, Dr. Karen returns to her proper place in the scheme of things, someone whose husband tells her what to do.

Now, Dr. Fred and Dr. Karen are the same age, and, once they are out of the hospital, the conventions of dominance are appropriately preserved. But what might happen to male dominance if the wife is mature, professionally successful, and older than her husband? The possibility, of course, is that she may dominate him.

A few years ago Swedish actress Liv Ullman starred in a movie called *40 Carats*. Ullman plays a businesswoman, many years divorced, who is just turning forty. On a vacation in Greece, she thumbs a ride with a young American on a motorcycle. They spend a passionate night together and she leaves early in the morning without waking him. We next see her in New York, going about her workaday life. One evening, her daughter brings in a new date for introductions. And the new date turns out to be the same young man of the idyllic Greek night. The young man pursues Ullman; they fall in love and he wants to marry her. She is hesitant; ultimately, love wins out.

The movie *40 Carats* was one of the earliest productions with the older woman/younger man theme. We noticed that the creators of this show definitively portrayed the young man as a rich, eminently successful businessman with an upper-class family background.

Although a proscribed cultural concept is being questioned

in this movie, all of the other conventions are carefully observed. The young man is presented as more successful, of higher social status, and, definitely, more decisive. Ullman may be older, but the young man will undoubtedly be the dominant partner in the relationship. The underlying message of the play is that a younger man/older woman relationship might be workable if the young man is richer, wiser, and one step ahead of the woman in the world: in other words, if he remains dominant. However, in real life, younger men are rarely in this position.

Since most societies have an established cultural belief that the right to dominate is derived from the power inherent in more years, more money, or higher status, people will assume that an older woman will dominate a younger man. If she possesses more of the accepted social symbols of power, a better job, property of her own or investments, the conventional power base in a relationship is reversed.

But the conventional symbols of power do not tell the whole story. The symbols represent one of the realities of the relationship, but there is an entire operation between power and dominance that takes place on another level. In spite of appearances to the contrary, neither the higher-achieving man nor the experienced older woman automatically dominates a relationship.

Actually, there is no human relationship without a power struggle. It is simply human nature for each individual in a relationship to be constantly maneuvering to be in control of the other's behavior. Author Jay Hailey, a communications analyst, explains the process as a perpetual attempt, on the part of each partner, to define the terms of the relationship. The object of these maneuvers is for each person to control the relationship to his or her own satisfaction.

"It should be emphasized here that control does not mean that one takes control of another person, as one would a robot. . . . Maneuvers to define a relationship consist essentially of (a) requests, commands, or suggestions that another person do, say, think or feel something; and (b) comments on the other person's communicative behavior."[2]

Hailey describes the maneuvering for control in a relationship as a process in which each person is continually trying to get one-up while keeping the other person one-down. However, when one person in a relationship has some kind of given social power, the fixed one-up and one-down positions are often accepted, at least for a while. Hailey refers to this kind of a relationship, in which two people are exchanging different kinds of behavior, as complementary.

In general, employer-employee, teacher-student, and parent-child relationships are complementary, because one person has more status than the other. If the person who is one-down accepts his or her status, these relationships have little conflict. The one-up position of the person who has the power — the employer, the teacher, or the parent — is taken mostly for granted. But as the person in the one-down position — the employee, the student, or the child — begins to develop confidence and competence, he or she will question the previously accepted power of the person in the one-up position and will begin his or her own maneuvering toward defining the terms of the relationship.

At this point, the person may be maneuvering for a symmetrical position, one in which the two persons exchange the same types of behavior. This is a competitive stance, which the person in the one-up position may not like. If the person in the one-up position insists on holding onto his or her complementary stance when the other person is requesting a change, a power struggle will ensue as the person who is one-down does everything he or she can do to become one-up. Since the male in our society, by virtue of custom, tradition, and training is considered permanently one-up on the female, the Hailey paradigm illustrates the power conflict typical of many male/female relationships.

We propose that a healthy relationship is one in which the positions of one-up and one-down readily shift according to human needs and life circumstances. It is absolutely natural for people to maneuver constantly for the higher position in the relationship. In the conventional marriage systems, however, it must at least appear that the man is one-up while the woman is one-down. As family therapists we know that the actuality is quite different. What is really going on is a long-term power struggle in which each person manipulates the other, consciously or unconsciously, to be one-up.

When the complementary system is rigidly enforced, some strange things can happen. We were told the story of a family where the husband rigorously controls all decisions, all money expenditure. In his opinion, his wife's function is cooking, cleaning, and caring for the children and himself. He finds the idea of his wife having time or an opinion for herself absolutely ridiculous. However, most of the time his wife is in bed with a mysterious nerve ailment. Almost all of her husband's money is spent on hospitals, expensive diagnostic testing, doctors, and nurses as well as someone to do the cooking, cleaning, and caring for the children and himself. He can barely call his life his own, but he dares not complain; after all, his wife is helpless; or is she? Who is really one-up in this situation?

Since our cultural conventions insist that the one with greater power (usually the man) should dominate the relationship, people assume that older women dominate younger men because greater age and experience in life are sources of power. Besides, the woman is often a strong, independent sort with a career and sometimes money of her own. So people think her poor little fellow shuffles along saying, "Yes, dear." That's not quite the way it works. Remember that both parties contest for power in all relationships; the older woman/ younger man relationship is not intrinsically different from any others.

During our interviews with older woman/younger man couples, normal maneuvering for control was observable. Of course, there was conflict. In any situation where two individuals are trying to coexist, the only time there is zero conflict is when they are both dead. But as we queried the older woman/younger man couples on the most intimate details of their lives, we often saw that relatively little energy was given over to intense power struggles.

As family therapists, we feel that our major tasks are to help people minimize crippling conflict, maximize comfort, and get on with their lives. Since we are used to observing extreme tension-producing maneuvers in relationships, we are always interested in how couples who cope well with each other manage their lives. Only a few of the people we interviewed for this book had any experience with family therapy, but most of them seemed to have figured out some effective ways to be comfortable with each other. Did they know something special about managing relationships?

The people we were interviewing had the usual number of hang-ups, foibles, and personal quirks. As individuals, they had the same day-to-day problems as other individuals. As couples, they not only faced the same worries that any other couple did, but they coped with the additional stress of being in an older woman/younger man relationship. Yet they seemed to handle life well, even enthusiastically. When we asked them, one by one, if they thought their relationships were different in any way from other marriages, many told us they knew something was better but they weren't always quite sure what it was.

These were some of the comments they offered: "I think it's because this relationship is easier for me. We don't seem to struggle with each other as much as my first husband and

I did." "We really care about what the other person thinks and does. We help each other a lot." "We don't compete; we cooperate."

As we went deeper into the details of their personal interactions, we discovered that these couples had a style of relating that limited the struggle for the one-up position. Older women/younger men relationships are not exempt from the controlling process. These are normal human beings who want what they want when they want it just like anyone else. But the influences on their personal lives are often different from those of conventional couples of the same age. The result is that a number of the couples we've interviewed have developed alternative ways of handling the struggle for power. In order to explain those influences and take a look at how they affect the older woman/younger man relationship, we have to recount a recent bit of history.

During the last forty years there have been a number of significant events that have deeply affected the life choices of both men and women in our society. A long period of economic prosperity, the inclusion of large numbers of women in the work force, the threat of overpopulation and the acceptance of zero population growth as a goal, and the impact of the women's movement have all contributed to opening up an era of immense personal freedom for both men and women. These recent changes in the way our society functions have opened up some fresh options for relationships. In particular, the evolution of the women's movement has drastically changed the conventional expectations of marriage.

The advent of the women's movement directly affects traditional sex roles. The move toward equality is both socially and economically influenced. It starts in the American school system, where the education of males and females is almost identical. Equal education breeds the idea that women should be treated as equals in a work situation. As a result, women are asking for equal pay for equal work, and they also want equal opportunity for advancement. Women are now seeking political power to achieve their aims. In addition, they are assuming traditionally male roles as bosses, supervisors, and professionals. A woman who has reached this level of self-development eventually will not accept anything less than equal power in a relationship. Author and teacher Susan Howard, forty-six, explains the dichotomy she experienced in her life ten years ago: "About that time I began to realize that I was one person in the office and another person at home. At work, I was somebody. My ideas, advise, and expertise were constantly sought. I made decisions, chaired meetings, and implemented plans. Actually, I did a lot of organizing and implementing at home, too, but I still felt like at least two faces of Eve. My department chairperson, who is also a close personal friend, was puzzled by my personality changes. One day he said to me, 'At work, you're dynamic and entirely in charge of yourself. At home you're a passive little mouse.' I got tired of feeling like a split personality and went into therapy. I emerged, some three years later, a lot more integrated and no longer married. Today, I will not accept a relationship in which I don't have equal rights and equal power. I don't have to be one-up, but I won't be one-down."

Male roles in our society are also affected by social change. The male's social message is to strive for dominance in every situation. As a result men have a tough time sharing power. They tend to compete instead of cooperating. Everything is a win-or-lose situation. In addition, many men cannot tolerate what they consider masculine characteristics in a female, such as assertiveness or leadership ability. There is some indication, however, that the traditional masculine attitude is becoming more flexible.

This change is occurring predominantly in men under forty. The radicalization of the sixties influenced new male perceptions of the social norms. Many young men are dissatisfied with the contemporary male image, the intense drive for success combined with the lack of intimate relationships with women *or* men. They are questioning the validity of so-called masculine behavior, values, and goals.

Herb Goldberg, teacher, psychotherapist and author of *The Hazards of Being Male*, warns that ". . . the male has paid a heavy price for his masculine 'privilege' and power. . . . He is a cardboard Goliath precariously balanced and on the verge of toppling over if he is pushed ever so slightly out of his well worn path."[3]

Androgynous behavior is a significant result of recent social changes. Social change for women leads to the development of so-called masculine personality traits, such as emotional independence, decision-making ability, sexual assertiveness, and more authoritative behavior in general. For this kind of woman, the primarily nurturing and dependent role no longer fits.

Social changes for men lead to the development of so-called feminine qualities. Some men want to complete the more human parts of themselves. They allow themselves to admit openly their need for nurturing. They recognize their own intuitive and emotional abilities. Many men want to be nurturing and supportive. They place a high value on intimacy, relationships, and family.

Most of the older women and younger men we interviewed tend to be androgynous whether they espouse traditional roles or flexible marriage styles. Androgyny is *not* role reversal. Role reversal would simply result in the same kind of power struggle. Specifically, androgyny is role expansion. To us, an androgynous person is one who combines both male and female roles. He or she is willing to give up the idea of certain inalienable sex-linked behaviors and find more productive solutions for living with another person. An androgynous man is more willing to cooperate and less anxious to compete or control in a relationship.

A large number of the men and women who chose older woman/younger man relationships tended toward role flexibility in their behavior and philosophy. As a result there was little emphasis on ensuring the man a one-up position.

But creating a relationship in which the power is shared is not an easy task even in an older woman/younger man relationship. The man has been raised in a culture where he is automatically given power by virtue of his gender. Even role flexibility and a desire to expand his softer self will not stop him from feeling uneasy about giving up the dominant position.

In the *Newsweek* article entitled "How Men Are Changing," the writers state, "The habits of male supremacy are deeply ingrained. Some anthropologists maintain that historical evidence shows there has never been a society in which men did not dominate. . . ."[4] (This is not true.) Men struggle to adjust to the new rules, but their habitual need to dominate keeps breaking through. Michael Singer, thirty-seven, a West Coast writer and male therapist, says he went along with the ideas and rhetoric of the movement at first, mainly to avoid confrontation. But he realized his basic attitudes had not changed. "I still wanted to control, to have the power in every situation," he says.[5] Our culture does not accept women in a dominant position. For a man even to appear to give up the dominant role is culturally unacceptable, not only to men, but to women as well. Our society is so thoroughly conditioned to the concept of male dominance that many women would feel lost in a peer relationship.

Emily, forty-three, told us, "I had a relationship with a younger man. It felt fragmented. We had good sex and wonderful companionship, but something was missing. I liked him a lot, but I don't think I was in love with him." What is it that Emily didn't find her young man? Is it possible that she was missing someone to look up to, someone who knew more than she; someone who was superior to her and could tell her what to do?

Some of the people we have interviewed have not chosen role flexibility as a marriage style for themselves. Both husband and wife are more comfortable with the man taking the lead in the relationship. However, even the more traditional couples tell us what they expect from each other is fairly clearly defined from the start. Mike and Mary Bayer have a conventional marriage style where, at least for the moment, with a new baby to care for, their roles are largely traditional. But they communicated to us that their marriage is based on friendship, a deep and abiding respect for each other. They will try to avoid abusing the power accorded each through separate male and female role function. On that basis, decision making about everything is shared even if money making and home care are not. When Mike Bayer's mother was asked what she liked best about her thirty-nine-year-old daughter-in-law, she replied, "She knows herself and she knows what she needs and wants. And my son is the same way."

But over and over we observe one principle of the older woman/younger man relationship, no matter whether the couple is flexible or traditional in their roles. Just the fact that the woman is older, more experienced, and, possibly, more accomplished than the man *neutralizes* the tendency for the man to dominate.

For instance, when a male and female who are contemporaries interact, the male, who by tradition is one-up, expects, and is usually given, more respect. But we are also culturally trained to give more respect to people who are older, more experienced, and more accomplished. So when an older woman interacts with a younger man, she won't automatically slot him into the one-up position; after all, he is her junior, and he doesn't necessarily expect to be one-up. On his side, because he is conditioned to respect her seniority, he won't initially try to maneuver her into the one-down position. Each one, at the very inception of the relationship, defines its terms as a peer situation, and each behaves toward the other as an equal. Since friendships usually take place between people who consider each other equals, the friendship becomes the foundation of their developing relationship.

The result is that although the tendency to expect the one-up position is built into the male through social conditioning, the man in the older woman/younger man relationship will not readily attempt to take the dominant position. If, in addition, a man prefers an expanded sex role, he does not equate dominance with his sexual identity as a male. With an attitude of mutual respect, and neither one seeking the one-up position on a permanent basis, the couple can proceed to develop their relationship as equals.

A thirty-eight-year-old businesswoman talks about how she and her husband, twenty-eight, share the power in their marriage. "I don't know who dominates. It's not him and it's not me. It feels pretty equal. He has power over his life; I have power over mine. We both take one another's wishes and feelings into account when making decisions. We both support one another's career goals. I honestly believe he'd never pull rank on me if I wanted to do something that would interfere with his needs. When I say pulling rank, I mean that he would tell me his needs are more important than mine, and that, as a woman, I should adapt. It's difficult enough to be a successful businesswoman without having a husband who undercuts your every move. I gave up my power to my first husband. There were several bad investments I let him go ahead with, when I knew better and it was my money. I'll never again be so foolish. I have a good mind for business and money management, and my present husband respects my judgment. I don't believe I dominate him, though I certainly do have an influence on him. The main thing is that he doesn't dominate me. I'm real tired of the 'I'm the man and I know best' routine. I've had it with that behavior. My husband listens, makes suggestions; I very much appreciate his contributions. He does a marvelous job of helping me sort out my thoughts without trying to impose his will."

Some of the people we interviewed shared power by freely letting go of conventionally male tasks like decision making and money handling. A number of the younger men we spoke to were more than content to give up some of their role tasks to the older women. They were aware that they chose to not be in charge of traditionally male areas of life.

A twenty-six-year-old writer, who has been living with a forty-eight-year-old teacher for four years, told us that he felt he has chosen to relinquish a great deal of control, which he can have back anytime he wants it. He moved into his lover's apartment and he moved into her life-style as well. He originally felt that when it came to clash points it was more appropriate to adopt an element of her life-style and her pattern rather than adopt his. "I was in a transition period of my life," he said, "and didn't have much pattern developed anyway." Issues that he would normally expect control to be based on — handling of money, organization of living routines, what kinds of activities they chose and when and how to do them — were largely handled by the woman he lives with. Most of the time she handles those things because she likes to and he doesn't. "But," he told us, "the new thing I've learned is that if I don't agree with the decision, I can speak up and have every right to be involved in those decisions without any power struggle."

Some women in older woman/younger man relationships are more traditional in their expectations than others, but the degree of control allowed is clearly specified. Tina Carey, a

forty-seven-year-old business executive, explains how her relationship with eleven-year-younger David works: "I'm very
competitive, but I don't think we fight for dominance because
I let him have it. I'm still a fifties girl in relationships; I don't
mind being told what to do. I feel I always have the option
of saying I don't want to do something. If I have an idea of
what I want to do, I will do it. I tend to let David make the
decisions, but he is aware of the fact that I reserve the right
to say no. I'd just as soon have somebody else figure out what
we're going to do tonight and he seems to enjoy that."

Tina's comments reflect a very important aspect of power
sharing, the ability to state clearly what one does and does not
want to do, most particularly when one feels strongly about
the action. When one person is not willing to let another
person know what's going on with him or her, the uninformed
partner can only make helpless guesses in an attempt to an-
ticipate the other's needs or wishes. And God help the partner
if he or she guesses wrong! The degree to which one partner
respects and acts on the information given by the other partner is the degree to which the relationship will be a trusting
one.

Tina told us that David is very open about what he wants
to do and when he wants to do it. Her ex-husband did not
have that kind of openness and Tina found it very hard to
negotiate with him. "He was full of defenses and strange in-
articulateness," she said, "so I never knew what the hell was
going on in our relationship." With David, however, Tina
feels pretty clear. It is an enormous relief to her to know what
she wants, what David wants, and what they want from each
other.

Although Tina feels that her relationship with David is a
fairly conventional one, they attempt to define their personal
boundaries clearly. Their roles are flexible to the degree that
Tina and David are comfortable with the arrangement.

Another potential conflict in a relationship can arise when two very powerful personalities struggle for control. Intensely dynamic people tend to create relationships in which the normal tension level is high. This is more likely to characterize an older woman/younger man relationship than any other.

Seth Shaler, thirty-one, is an attorney married to Kelly Watson, thirty-nine, a senior executive with a major movie studio. They have been together for eight years. They discussed their often tempestuous relationship with us.

Seth told us, "We are two immensely powerful people. In my entire life I have never met anybody I could not dominate except for Kelly, which is not to say that I want to dominate her or that she dominates me. Obviously, in powerful people there is an urge to be a dominant force, but there is a mitigating dynamic between us; I can acquiesce to her getting away from my control because I trust her judgment a lot.

"One of the things that attracted me is the fact that she is a strong woman. I have never found any woman attractive who was not powerful. And I've never been able to deal for more than fifteen minutes with being with a woman who wasn't powerful. We feel that it is necessary for powerful people to work out a system that engenders a balance of power; otherwise there is no relationship. There is only a continual struggle. That's not a tolerable situation as far as I'm concerned."

Seth had barely paused when Kelly took over: "I'm very strong-willed and I've never been able to be in a situation with men where I was the weak partner. I'm very willful and tough-minded. I have all the characteristics of being a first child and being dominant in my family. I despise people who operate only from a position of weakness. So it's impossible for me to be in a situation where I don't have equality. I've always had trouble with men who wanted women to be charms on their arms. I could have married a rich man and been taken care of, but I never did it, never liked it; never liked the feeling. Seth and I are partners. We both work hard in very competitive situations."

Both Seth and Kelly, as professionals, are expected to exercise their naturally authoritative personalities, their leadership abilities, and their decision-making capacities on a daily basis. It would be impossible for two such strongly determined people to live together without some clash of will; their conversational style alone resembles a tennis match at Wimbledon, two champions going at each other for all they are worth. Seth and Kelly recognize that part of their attraction is the challenge each represents to the other. They also need to realize that if they stay embattled all of the time, the goodwill of their marriage will be exhausted.

As we went about interviewing older woman/younger man couples, we looked very carefully at the way the struggle for power and/or dominance was manifested in these relationships. We found a variety of styles of coping with power struggles. We met older woman/younger man couples where both partners conceded that the man had more decision-making power. These couples were usually in open agreement about their respective roles in the relationship. But over half of the couples we interviewed told us their partnership was essentially equal, with power flowing from one to the other as circumstances warranted.

On several occasions when we asked couples which one of them dominated the relationship, we got answers that revealed a great deal about what was going on. In one case, the younger man, in a separate interview, told us that he thought he dominated the relationship. Later, when we asked his older wife the same question, she smiled. "I'm sure he thinks he does," she said, "but I know that I am every bit as valuable to him as he is to me. If it pleases him to think that he has more power in the relationship, that's okay. Down deep, he really doesn't." This particular wife is willing to give the one-up position to her husband if he needs it, to make him happy. Since she is satisfied that she is of equal importance in the relationship, this older woman can accede to her husband's desire to be one-up and eliminate a potential power struggle.

Another older woman/younger man couple's comments indicated a more conflicted situation. When we asked them who dominated the relationship, they quickly and simultaneously pointed to each other. Then they laughed. But the husband sighed when he said, "Mostly, I feel that she dominates. She's so much more expressive than I am." "I do talk a lot more," the wife responded, "but he can have equal say anytime. He just doesn't say what he wants very much." The thirty-year-old husband told us that he came from a taciturn family where nobody ever directly expressed thoughts or feelings. The wife, who is thirty-eight, is almost disconcertingly forthright about everything that she experiences.

As we continued the interview, we discovered that the wife was used to being in situations where feelings and ideas are controversially expressed, while her husband was just getting used to the fact that it was all right to venture a contradicting opinion in polite society. They told us that they saw their seven-year relationship as a partnership, but in a recent discussion had found out, with some shock, that the concept of partnership meant something totally different to each of them. At another point in the interview the husband said, "I don't always like all this discussion and working out of agreements, particularly when we can't seem to agree on what certain important things mean." His wife nodded. "Before we make an agreement, we certainly have to have something we both agree on."

Attitudes in common are not sufficient for a relationship. Specific requests have to be stated and clarified in order to negotiate an agreement. What each person wants out of the relationship has to be presented to the other in as much detail as possible. When either partner feels that the other has too much control in the situation, then each one is also struggling to get his or her share of the control back, whether or not either is consciously aware of it.

Strangely enough, one of the most common maneuvers to get more control is to leave the relationship. Withholding oneself is a threat to the other to behave in accordance with the partner's wishes or the misbehaving person will be abandoned. Unfortunately, this maneuver is often used prematurely, usually because the partner who is leaving doesn't know any other way to get back control of his or her life.

But if total control of the relationship is what the partner is really after, no amount of negotiation or agreement will change anything. The sharing of power involves relinquishing, once and for all, the idea that one person can control another. Negotiations and agreements replace the concept of single dominance.

Although it may appear to the untrained eye that the partner with more life experience may dominate in a marriage, when the relationship is examined closely, the other partner will be seen to be competing equally in his or her own way for control.

It is quite possible, however, that an older woman who is assertive might be experienced as dominating the couple. Equally often, the man might be perceived as submissive because he is not particularly aggressive. In addition, we are so totally unused to mutually cooperative behavior, as opposed to a competition for power, in a relationship that the very neutrality of the couple's interaction feels somehow out of kilter.

We think that older women and younger men are attracted to each other, in part, because they both prefer to share power, whether or not they are consciously aware of this predisposition. We see that many mid-life women are almost deliberately choosing younger partners for mates. There is often considerable emotional conflict between mid-life women and their male contemporaries, a conflict about power that is not always easily resolved. Certain women, particularly those who have reached a comfortable level of personal independence, prefer younger men as partners simply because there is less of a battle for supremacy.

A number of older women/younger men relationships are challenging the idea that one person must dominate a relationship. Several of our interviewees have developed a type of relationship that departs sharply from our cultural expectations. It is one in which both people expect equal participation in all parts of their lives from home and child care to earning the money. As full partners, they are trying to build an interdependent system that is quite different from the rigid dependency of many contemporary marriages.

One of the most significant factors in human relationships is the issue of power and how it is handled. In a mature relationship, desired behavior is requested, not coerced. The majority of the people whom we have interviewed are making a deliberate effort to move away from the power struggle. Influenced by social change, they are exercising alternative options to create a form of relationship in which power flows more easily from one partner to another.

7·

WHO'S LOOKING
FOR A MOTHER?

As FAMILY THERAPISTS WE SEE THAT BOTH PART-
ners in a relationship maneuver to get what they want from
each other. And often what each clearly desires is a measure
of caretaking from the other. Yet many people are convinced
that a younger man chooses an older woman as a mate because he needs to be mothered by her. And, according to current psychiatric thinking, not only is the younger man looking
for a mother in an older woman/younger man relationship
but the woman committed to a younger man is looking for
someone she can mother: that is, someone she can dominate
or control.

For instance, when actress Kate Jackson, thirty-one, married actor Andrew Stevens, seven years younger, journalists
rushed to get psychiatric opinions on the potential of the
marriage to succeed. The media psychiatrists uniformly perceived the relationship as neurotic and doomed from the
start.

"The prognosis for this marriage is zilch," declared one
psychiatrist. "In marrying a man who is almost seven years

her junior, what Kate Jackson is saying in effect is: I want to be looked up to and I don't want to depend on any man. ... I want to be the leader in the marriage. ..."[1]

In the same article, the medical director of a psychotherapy center was quoted, ". . . She chose a younger man, a man she can control. In marrying someone younger, she both assures herself and communicates to the world that she is and will be in charge — that she is going to make the decisions."[2]

By implication, a younger man is easily manipulable, a piece of putty in her hands, someone who will not struggle with her for the right to lead or the right to make decisions. A great many psychiatrists and psychologists would assert that the younger man involved with an older woman is an emotional weakling looking for a strong mother figure to give sustenance, structure, and direction to his life: in short, to dominate him. The validity of this idea needs to be seriously explored.

Psychoanalytic theory, in particular, proposes the idea that a young man who is attracted to an older woman is a person who has not yet given up the notion of marrying his mother. Insistence on a literal interpretation of the oedipal conflict theory presupposes that a relationship in which the woman is older than the man is automatically suspect. According to this idea, the emotional development of a man who marries an older woman is questionable. Psychologically speaking, he must be seeking a mother or why would he give up the position of dominance? Not so incidentally, the younger man is also making the woman unavailable to a man her own age, thereby symbolically stealing her away from the father figure.

Dr. Carl Jung, who was an early disciple of Freud but later developed his own theories, felt, however, that the oedipal conflict theory was more a metaphor about the stages of human development than a literal representation of neurosis. From the Jungian point of view, oedipal fixation, the desire to kill the father in order to gain the mother for oneself, represents the process each person, male or female, must go through in order to come to terms with him- or herself as a mature human being.

"Killing the father" symbolizes understanding our own particular programming, the ideas about life imposed on us by others when we were children, as differentiated from the need to live our lives based on our own separate and individual adult experiences of the world. "Gaining the mother" represents the desire of all human beings to have an all-protecting person who will give them anything they want, anytime they want it, and who will never let anything happen to them. Accepting the idea that this all-protective, all-nurturing person doesn't and never will exist is perhaps the most difficult achievement in life.

Still, most of us, both men and women, long for the metaphorical mother and often attempt to manipulate the other member of a relationship to perform that function. In order to understand this, let's take a look at what "looking for a mother" might mean in its everyday human sense. What, exactly, does a mother do? A mother is supposed to take care of you. She fixes meals, does your laundry, and kisses your hurts to make them well. She soothes and comforts. At best she guides or advises. At worst, she tells you what to do and interferes in your life. She attempts to teach you how to take care of yourself physically and emotionally. Small children think Mother has magical powers because Mother always knows when they have misbehaved. Mother can console and she can punish. The image is one of a woman who is powerful and remains a dominant figure in one's life.

This definition of a mother is a generalization that includes stereotypical ideas. Nevertheless, because mothers and wives often have similar functions, their separate identities tend to be fused into one concept. Mothers can definitely be punishing and powerful: that is, dominant. Wives can sometimes be punishing, but unlike a man's mother, should never be allowed to obtain a position of power and superiority in his life.

How do you keep a wife from being powerful? By making sure that she is not older than her husband. Mothers are women who are older. Since all of our mothers are older than we are, we take this fact for granted. When we were children, Mother, an older woman, was more powerful than we were. The assumption that if the woman is older than the man, she will have more power in the relationship is an unconscious carryover from childhood.

But what about a situation in which the man is publicly acknowledged as a young person of extraordinary business achievement? His respected position in the world often will free him from a negative assessment of his emotional development.

A case in point is the late Aristotle Socrates Onassis, international shipping tycoon, whose rollcall of wives and mistresses includes names like Jacqueline Kennedy Onassis and Maria Callas. One of the most significant relationships of Onassis's life, however, his twelve-year connection with Ingeborg Dedichen, has never been much publicized until recently. Ingeborg Dedichen, the daughter of one of Norway's wealthiest families, met Onassis when she was thirty-five and he was twenty-eight. For over a dozen years she lived with him in New York, Paris, and Greece, being hostess at his parties and sharing his life. Although at the time when they met, Onassis was already a multimillionaire, Ms. Dedichen's friends were aghast that she was willing to spend time with him. As wealthy and powerful as he was, Onassis, according to Ms. Dedichen's associates, was still unschooled in the etiquette and behavior of the very rich.

Ms. Dedichen's money was obviously not the object of the

relationship. Although Ingeborg Dedichen had formerly been very rich, at the time of her meeting with Onassis she was almost penniless. Her shipowner father was dead and she had little direct connection with the business world. What she had to offer Onassis was acceptance in the best circles of royal and international society. They fell in love, each magnetized by the other's immense personal charm. He proposed marriage; she repeatedly refused. When they ultimately parted ways, Onassis was over forty years old.

Often, when an older woman/younger man marriage is publicly announced, the media psychiatrists, as we've seen, inform us that the men involved in these relationships are defective males who need to find a strong mother figure to safeguard them from a cold, cruel world. Aristotle Onassis, from what is known of both his public and his private life, hardly fits this image. This man, in addition to being one of the most internationally powerful figures of our time, wooed and won a series of women who were international celebrities in their own right. For all of these women his attraction lay in his personality. In answer to her friends' criticism of the affair, Ingeborg Dedichen once said, "Although he was not in the least what you could call well-bred, you could sense his acute intelligence behind those dark, impish eyes, and when he smiled, he could charm mountains. He was all at once funny, tender and brutal. . . ."[3] From the biographical data available, Onassis's relationship with Ingeborg Dedichen simply doesn't fit the stereotype of a vapid youth in search of an extension of maternal reassurance.

Dr. Wayne Myers of New York Hospital was quoted in *Newsweek* as saying that younger men use this kind of relationship to build their confidence and then leave the older woman for a younger one. "Probably these men have been rejected by someone their own age and they fear another rejection," he explains.[4] If a younger man attempts a relationship with an older woman on the belief that a mother figure is less likely to reject him, he is bound to be disappointed. An older woman is far more likely to leave a younger lover than a man of her own age because conventional thinking tells her that there is no future in the relationship. In reality, we don't see the young man's looking for acceptance from an older woman as any more safe than attempting a relationship with someone his own age. Falling in love with anyone involves certain emotional risks.

What is the actual experience of the younger man in a relationship with an older woman? Does living with an older woman make life easier for him? Is the greater worldliness of the woman a real help to him? How does he see himself in the situation?

Nachmy Bronstein, a thirty-one-year-old Israeli, is married to Phyllis Chesler, psychologist, author and one of the most radically outspoken leaders of the women's movement. Ms. Chesler is ten years older than her husband. In a magazine interview, Bronstein was asked if he minded "that many people perceived his wife as more important than he."[5]

"First of all, she *is* more important," he admits. "I'm younger; she has accomplished much more. But our relationship is unique and I don't care what the outside world thinks, though it is painful when her friends come to our house and ignore me."[6]

Bronstein's comments are similar to those we have heard from other young men in relationships with older women. Often they are scorned by the woman's friends from a previous life. Sometimes the young men are snubbed; they are seen as a passing fancy that will disappear if disregarded. A young man who is highly sensitive to rejection is not the kind of person who can commit himself to an older woman. Disapproval of the relationship is intense, both from women and other men, who will see the younger man as the betrayer of the male code. The men who risk relationships with older women need to be able to take a lot of flak. Either they have the ego strength to "step to the music" of "a different drummer" or the relationship does not survive. This is a far different image of the younger man from the stereotype that is usually allowed.

While people assume that a younger man married to an older woman must be looking for a mother to take care of him, no one thinks that an older man or even one the same age as his wife could possibly be in the same position. There is no question that some men do seek out women to mother them, to make their decisions and take responsibility for their lives. But in our clinical practice we have observed that this behavior does not necessarily have anything to do with the man's age or that of his wife. The traditional male image notwithstanding, human beings of both sexes are capable of giving up their independence in exchange for the protection and care of another. Certain kinds of men and women automatically do this in a relationship, accepting domination by the other in return for a measure of supportiveness.

This is not necessarily the case with older woman/younger man couples, but in order to explore this belief we have to go back to our definition of "mothering." Mothers are powerful and nurturing; Mothers also control and punish. If a man seeks nurturing, which in our society is confused with mothering, then he might also have to accept punishment and control. Our childhood experiences link these two maternal behaviors together. Therefore, a man with an older woman is suspect. He is seen as a person who will accept being controlled by a woman in exchange for emotional support.

In addition, it is not acceptable for an adult to need mothering. An adult looking for mothering must be childish or immature. This goes double for a grown man. A real man takes care of himself; he doesn't depend on anyone else.

Agreement with this premise means that any human need a grown person has for love, caring, and nurturing is interpreted as neurotic.

We do not agree with the premise stated above. In clinical practice we see that human beings need continuing emotional support from others throughout their lives, in addition to their own self-sufficiency. If they don't get it, they are apt to be sad, malfunctioning people. Consistent lack of nurturance from others contributes to the breakdown of physical and emotional welfare. The result is that a male in our society, who is supposed to do the controlling and not be controlled, is placed in a double bind. How can he get his emotional needs met without also accepting the control of the woman who nurtures him?

In order to get out of the cycle of controlling and being controlled by others, a person must be able to differentiate between a basic human need for emotional support and being helplessly dependent. Unfortunately, the lines between childish dependency and adult interdependency are often blurred. For instance, the kind of parental nurturing style that grown men and women ordinarily impose on each other consists of giving explicit instructions about how to make the other's life work. In this system, each partner always knows what is best for his or her mate. A nurturing style between peers is quite different. It might be described as the willingness to listen to the other person's problems, give physical comfort when necessary, make suggestions if asked, and, possibly, be available when needed.

The difference in these two types of behavior is distinct. In the first instance, the marriage partners take full responsibility for making decisions about each other's personal lives as one would with a child. In the second instance, each partner makes his or her own decisions and each one is also empathetic to the life situation of the other. The primary activity of a parental style is telling the other what to do; the basic behavior of an adult style is carefully listening.

Traditionally, it has been considered unmanly for grown males to admit openly a need for nurturing. However, even without admitting it, men continually try to get nurturing in any way they can. Since most men do not nurture other men, the obvious place to seek emotional support is from a woman. That, however, would be soliciting mothering, so if a real man is to get nurtured, it must be by an indirect, roundabout approach, with both the man and the woman in tacit agreement not to notice what has taken place. Since everybody is busy pretending that the man doesn't really need nurturing, after a while the woman starts feeling cheated about not having her services acknowledged. In time, when the man circuitously comes back for more unacknowledged nurturing, he will be turned away.

It is more acceptable for a woman to ask for emotional support from a man, but what she usually gets instead is overprotectiveness, a parental behavior that assumes that the woman is incapable of thinking or acting for herself and must be told what to do. If the woman continues to try to get nurturing from her husband, he will respond by giving her more patronizing advice and then pull away in frustration because she won't do what he tells her.

It should not be surprising that the same kind of behavior, in reverse, often occurs in the older woman/younger man relationship. After all, we are given the option to model only two kinds of behavior, male or female. In this situation, the older wife behaves the same way the traditional husband does. She reacts impatiently to the lower level of experience of her younger mate in the same way that a husband may give short shrift to his wife's experiencing the world differently from him. For example, when a husband tells a wife that the solution to her problem is to assert herself more, and she does not know what assertion is, she is likely to feel that she has asked for help and received none at all.

If a woman is frequently irritated by a man's being guilty of nothing more serious than being younger than she, then an older woman/younger man relationship is probably not a good idea for her. For instance, a younger man may be newly fumbling with adult social skills at which she has been an expert for years. Criticism and offhand advice on how easy they are seem condescending and worthless. The support and encouragement of the younger man's developing abilities will be much more appreciated.

In many same-age marriages, each partner functions only in the role that the conventions of the society give to him or her. Men are the thinkers and doers, while women are the only available nurturers. As a result, grown persons can easily become stuck in a parent/child dependency on each other. Each tries to control the other's behavior in order to receive caretaking. Even though it may appear that the man dominates the relationship, the reality is that he is working endlessly to keep control of his supply of nurturance.

The parent/child dependency will also occur in relationships in which the woman attempts to dominate a man. It is not unusual for women to try dominating even in marriages where the man is the same age or older. Female one-upmanship is definitely not limited to the older woman/younger man relationship. However, the psychological basis of an attempt to dominate is always the same in male or female: lack of self-confidence linked with fear of abandonment. Both men and women are frightened by the possibility of loss of love.

Family therapists offer a variety of ways for a couple to get out of the painful cycle of using controlling behavior in order to elicit caring from each other. One of those ways is to encourage each partner to expand his or her concept of his or her own role. Women are capable of logical thought and giving sound advice and men are feeling human beings who deserve comforting and cuddling and are capable of giving both.

As the older woman/younger man couples shared their ideas of what male and female meant to them, we discovered that most of the people responded with enthusiasm to the idea of role expansion. Their discussions with us indicated that development of masculine and feminine life skills for both partners was an important part of their lives. Says Susan Howard, forty-six, "In addition to being a teacher and a writer, I have highly developed feminine skills, including child care, homemaking, and the ability to comfort and reassure friends who are going through a bad patch. Anything I can do Peter can do equally well. I am so proud to have a man who can be my equal in achievement *and* in nurturing."

Role flexibility allows both men and women to admit human error, disappointment, and the need for comforting. Emotional openness gives each person a chance to nurture the other more effectively. The result is that people can let go of controlling behavior. When a man or a woman can receive comfort and reassurance just for the asking, there is no need to waste energy on setting up an elaborate system of dominance. Within a mutually supportive framework, nurturance is easily available to both partners.

As we have pointed out earlier in the chapter, the traditional male's idea of nurturing is to give a woman the protection of his superior thinking ability and greater earning power. These may not meet the needs of today's woman. She can already think for herself and she makes money quite competently. What she still needs in her life is a partner with whom she can share friendship and emotional supportiveness.

Marian Alexander, thirty-nine, who was interviewed by

Ebony for an article entitled "Older Women — Young Men," says that she can relate much better to younger men than to those her own age because she feels that younger men are more sensitive to her emotional needs. Ms. Alexander stated: "I don't need someone to provide me with food, shelter and clothing; I can provide these for myself. I need emotional security, and a whole lot of Black men my age just can't provide me with that, whereas a younger man can. Some men about my age haven't made the transition from yesteryear to today. They feel threatened by women contemporaries who are professional. When you meet a man, the hostilities immediately come out. You have to be friends before you can be lovers. . . . The young man is more open-minded. . . . He came up in a different social structure and he has a different attitude."[7]

Ms. Alexander's words reflect the attitude of a number of the women we have interviewed who are in relationships with younger men. What these women want is a more flexible attitude toward their personal goals, something that is often difficult to find with men their own age.

A forty-eight-year-old novelist told us, "In the fifteen years of my adult life that I have not been married, I have had lovers who were friends and friends who were lovers. They have been my age, older, and younger. I do not choose to marry again, but if I did, it might be to a younger man. It is simply less exhausting to set up a mutual support system with a man who is younger and less fixed in his ways."

A woman who has grown into her full potential as a person and who can take care of herself is likely to have problems with any man, older, younger, or the same age, who has rigid definitions of the male and female roles. Role flexibility is not essential to an older woman/younger man relationship, but many people who have talked to us feel that it is very important. Flexibility is particularly conducive to the flow of nurturance between two people, largely eliminating the struggle for dominance and engendering supportiveness for both partners.

Phyllis Chesler, forty-one, is author of *Women and Madness,* co-author with Emily Goodman of *Women, Money and Power.* Her book *About Men* is a scathing denunciation of the behavior of the male sex. Yet *About Men* is dedicated to Ms. Chesler's husband, Nachmy Bronstein, thirty-one, "who has blessed me with his gentleness and beauty."[8] In an interview Ms. Chesler was asked how she could reconcile this loving dedication with her bleak perception of men. "I dedicated the book to him," she said to the interviewer, "not because he is a man or he is my husband, but because when I was writing it, he was my mother. The 'good' men, the ones who are struggling for something different, are very few. And I bless them. They are very new and very fragile. They are finding out that they must cut their ties with the rewards of being men. They are scared, and sometimes they are not sure they are doing the right thing. Most do not have other male feminist friends, and they cannot go back to their other friends."[9]

Nachmy Bronstein, Ms. Chesler says, "respects me more than anyone else who knows me. He knows when I'm scared and he knows to hug me. He knows the importance of creature comfort, continuity, stability."[10]

"He mothers me." In almost every interview that statement has echoed from the lips of women who have married or who live with younger men. "He respects me; he likes what I do and who I am. He nurtures me." Our interviewees tell us that while some younger men do look for someone to take charge of their lives, just as young women do, men in relationships with older women are not necessarily looking for mothers. What a number of women have reported to us, in fact, is that the men are doing their share, and more, of the nurturing.

During our interviews women said on several occasions,

"This is the first man I've ever been with who really takes care of me." A woman who makes this comment has often come from a long-term first marriage where she was her husband's support and helpmeet and was responsible for raising several children. Her history consists of years and years of caretaking during which no one took care of her. Granted, during that time of her life she was not willing to give up the one power that her culture allowed her: the power of being the only one who could take care of others. Having others dependent on her for all emotional support gave her the only area of dominance in her family. Allowing someone else actually to take care of her, in the comforting, nurturing way that she took care of others, would eliminate her dominance in that area.

The result is that the woman who has been the hyper-responsible wife and mother for the first part of her adult years has also systematically deprived herself of that kind of care. Consequently, when she gets to the stage of development where she can give up being the all-encompassing care-taker, she is deeply appreciative and at times astounded by her younger partner's willingness to give emotional and physical nurturing. Here are some of the comments made by women with younger husbands on the subject of nurturing:

"He actually gets up in the middle of the night to get me a drink of water."

"When I'm sick, he brings me meals in bed — his version of chicken soup, which is soft-boiled egg with bits of toast in it. If I have a headache, he'll put a cold cloth on my head. When I had surgery, he was in the room when I awoke because he knows I'm scared of anesthesia. He changed my nightgown and cleaned up my bed."

"If I'm upset, he'll ask if I want to talk about it. Then he'll listen and help me sort it all out. I can tell him about my professional problems. He doesn't criticize or advise. He's a good sounding board and he thinks my work is important. That means a lot to me."

The younger men we've interviewed admit that they want and are willing to accept nurturing from their older women partners. Seth, a thirty-one-year-old lawyer whose wife is eight years older, told us, "I don't need Kelly to fix my meals or decorate my house. I can do that just fine. What I need is the support she gives me. We both work in tough, competitive jobs. When we come home we comfort and encourage one another."

A twenty-six-year-old gas company repairman, married to a thirty-five-year-old woman, told us: "There are times when I feel very upset and confused about myself or some part of my life. When that happens I know that my wife is there for me. I might need her to listen to my feelings; I might need her to hold me; I might need reassurance; I might need her to take over some of my responsibilities temporarily. She doesn't panic. She doesn't look down on me because I'm not totally together. She accepts my humanness. It's a great relief."

Nurturance is the ability to offer comfort, caretaking, or support. It is helpful to tell your partner what kind of nurturance you need. Open communication prevents the uncertain process of guessing. A parent gives a child the kind of care the parent believes the child needs. But adults have enough life experience to know what they want, even though they sometimes don't have the assertiveness to ask for it.

As a type of behavior, assertion is power in action. In relationships, assertiveness is the ability to impact on or influence another person and get a response. The response reinforces the asserter's sense of being important in the life of the other. When partners sabotage assertive behavior in each other, they are cultivating dependent behavior. When they encourage assertiveness, they are creating interdependency, a relationship between adults who are equals.

Many people choose to believe that if their partner really loved them, a request for nurturing should be unnecessary. Somehow, the other person should magically know when and how the partner required expressions of caring. When the magic isn't working, which often happens, the manipulations for control come into play in an attempt to get the desired response. Without assertive behavior, usually in the form of direct requests, there is little chance of developing a mutually nurturing support system.

Psychologist Rollo May, on the subject of giving nurturance, describes this ability as a form of power. He explains nurturance as "power for the other." "Obviously," he says, "a good deal of this kind of power is necessary and valuable in relations with friends and loved ones. It is the power that is given by one's care for the other; we wish him well."[11] This is power we often see in the older woman/younger man relationship. Nurturing power is accepted as a position of strength for both women and men. It is clearly not a position of weakness.

In our interviews we have heard several stories that describe the nurturance that older women and younger men give each other and, on occasion, the sacrifices they are willing to make to assist each other's lives. Traditionally, men have always expected this behavior from women, but most of the older woman/younger man couples we have met strongly support each other.

And Peggy Randall, forty-nine, does it a little differently. She both supports and shares her thirty-six-year-old husband's work goals and his work life. Doug is a minister with a demanding professional schedule. Peggy is delighted to be able to share Doug's career, not only fulfilling her functions as the minister's wife, but actively encouraging Doug to follow in the directions his heart and conscience take him. "I'm glad Peggy feels this way about my being a minister," Doug said, "because it really takes the two of us to do this one job properly. If Peggy wasn't willing to contribute her brains, her skills with people, her empathy, and her warmth to sharing this job with me, I'd be perpetually suffering from nervous exhaustion. By working together, we enjoy ourselves and get to spend more time together." The Randalls told us that the ministry can be intensely stressful even to very good marriages. Peggy feels strongly that by the combining of her strengths with Doug's, rather than her having a separate profession, their relationship can become even more close. "Actually," she grinned, "I love being able to share in his ministry."

Couples can help each other go through developmental stages with a mutual support system. Paul Stefano, for instance, has financially supported his wife, Liz, while she finished graduate school and her internship as a psychologist. "I am waiting until Liz's practice is established," he told us, "and then I will start my own career transition."

Support of a partner's career goals is not always easy. One fifty-two-year-old woman travels extensively in her job as a buyer for a chain of department stores. Her husband, thirty-five, doesn't particularly care for the fact that she is away for a part of each month. "But there are so many women who capably hold down the fort while their husbands put in travel time as part of their jobs," he said, "and I would hate to think I can't handle myself as well as they do." Not liking the circumstances is understandable, but having the goodwill to adjust to them because of a partner's career demands is highly nurturing.

Al, fifty-three, and Jane, sixty-four, have a particular problem. Jane has reached retirement age and is ready to take off on the one-year camper trip around the United States that she and Al have been planning for some time. For Al, leaving his job at the age of fifty-three is risking his livelihood. Yet, if he waits too long, Jane may not be physically capable of sharing an active retirement. Al has decided that he will quit his job and go on that trip with Jane. While Al may be taking a chance by leaving his job now, they agree that waiting until Al's retirement would be a greater risk to their future together.

The choices these couples have made not only point out the partners' support of each other but, even more important, emphasize effective support of the relationship itself. Often, while one person in a marriage is moving toward his or her respective life goals, the other partner's desires and dreams are forced into the background, causing the relationship to suffer. One interviewee told us that shortly before her marriage broke up, her ex-husband had said to her, "I think the problem is that I want to do what I want to do and I also want *you* to do what *I* want you to do. And I know that you're not going to do that anymore." Primarily, in our interviews, we found an attitude of mutual encouragement, a sense of working together toward separate goals. This "power for the other" was expressed by one younger husband when he explained, "I want to help my wife get whatever she wants for herself and I know she'll stand by me the same way."

In all too many relationships, nurturing is sought by indirect means. Both partners are manipulated, often with resentment as a consequence, into sex, into caretaking, into supportiveness, into paying attention to the other one in thousands of different ways, whether they want to or not. The whole performance is reminiscent of the demands that children make continually on their mothers and on their fathers when they are available.

Of course, younger men behave childishly sometimes, and so do younger women, and older women and older men, as well. But who is really looking for a mother? We all are; older women, older men, younger women and younger men, in the sense that all human beings seek mothering, at least the warmth, comfort, and acceptance that mothering symbolizes. Nurturance is a lifetime need for both men and women and not exclusive to childhood. And the ability to nurture is not restricted to a single sex. Human beings of both sexes have the ability to give each other emotional support in the form of attention, respect, and patience. Male sexual identity does not have to be defined as the withholding of simple acts of human kindness, a soothing word, holding a loved one close, or an empathetic response to someone else's pain. A woman does not have to lose her sexual identity as a caring person by thinking clearly, carving out a career, and not letting everyone walk all over her.

In the older woman/younger man relationship there is the potential for just being human with ample mothering available for all. In our search for the ways in which older woman/younger man relationships might be similar or different from others, we found that a high level of mutual nurturance turned out to be a significant benefit enjoyed by these couples.

As family therapists, committed to the concept of helping marriage work, we have learned a great deal from older woman/younger man relationships about how the role of mutual nurturance can help a relationship to endure.

8 ·

MONEY AND STATUS

AT THE END OF THE CHAPTER ON POWER AND DOMInance we mentioned that one of the keys to a successful relationship is that power can flow freely from one partner to the other. In our society, money and status are equated with power. According to social convention, as we've said, the man in a relationship should have more power — that is, more money and status — than the woman, but in this area the older woman/younger man relationship is most atypical, since, in many cases, the woman has more money and more status than the man. We are going to examine the ways and extent to which this is a problem to the older woman/younger man relationship.

Several of the women we interviewed have more money than their younger men partners. They either earn more or they have acquired more money because they are older. When an older woman has more money than her younger husband, comments about both of them are likely to be derogatory. The woman is usually perceived as foolish. She is putting herself in a position to be taken advantage of. Regardless of whatever financial arrangements the couple has made for themselves, gossip will have it that the younger man is living off the woman's money. Even if he is tidily managing on his own smaller income, people will wonder what kind of man he is and what his real motives are in marrying an older woman.

Speculation about the financial motives of a younger man marrying a well-to-do older woman are a relatively recent phenomenon. It is only within the last hundred years and in limited places in the world that married women have been allowed to retain legal rights to their own property. Up until then a wife's money became the husband's legal property as soon as the wedding took place. Before a woman had the protection of the law in regard to her money and property, a wealthy older woman was considered quite a catch for a younger man. In an earlier time, people didn't suspect that a man was marrying an older woman for her money; they took it for granted.

For instance, Geoffrey Chaucer, in *The Canterbury Tales*, tells about Alice, a forty-year-old widow from the city of Bath. Alice has had five husbands. The last one was twenty years younger than she. But Alice has outlived them all. She is independently wealthy, having inherited money and property from her spouses. In addition, she is a weaver by profession and has a thriving business. The lady may be getting on, but she has a lusty disposition, a fine sense of humor, and considerable income. And what she wants most is another husband, preferably a young and healthy one who can satisfy her sexually.

Chaucer implies that Dame Alice will not remain a widow for long. The man who marries her will take legal possession of her investments, savings, and earnings as well as her robust sexuality. Mayhap he will get more than he bargained for, but in the fourteenth century, it would have been a fair trade.

Even today, there are modern cultures that do not allow

married women to retain legal control of their money. A colleague told us about a seventy-year-old woman friend in Switzerland who is currently seeking a divorce from her fifty-five-year-old husband. According to Swiss law, if this woman divorces her husband, everything she has, inheritances from her family, her savings, and even her earnings as a well-known artist, will belong to her husband. Regardless of what she decides to do, her younger husband retains all financial control in the situation.

But in many modern societies a woman can continue to control her own income after marriage. As a result, when a younger man chooses an older woman to be his mate, people assume that the source of attraction is money and that she is going to support him. Obviously, this is the reverse of conventional arrangements in marriage and, since it is, society has established a category for this behavior. Because the woman has legal control of her money, the man is, to all intents and purposes, her gigolo.

What most of us know about the function of a gigolo is rather vague. Are his liaisons simply sexual or are they emotionally involved as well? What is the nature of the arrangement between a gigolo and his mistress? Does she take care of him or does he take care of her? Specifically, what — or who — is a gigolo?

According to a recent book, *Gigolo*, he is a man who is financially supported by a woman in exchange for playing a rigidly defined role in her life. He is expected to be a charming, witty, well-groomed companion at all times and to be on call as a competent lover. He cannot work or have other interests because he must be available when the woman needs him. Being a gigolo is a full-time job.

Who are the women who might choose to employ a gigolo, a man who is, in essence, nothing more menacing than a paid companion? Some might lack confidence in their ability to interest men. Others might be unwilling to risk the pain of emotional involvement. The employer-employee relationship sharply limits both mutuality and intimacy.[1]

The rules of this kind of relationship are actually very strict. The roles of a gigolo and his mistress are not flexible. Under no circumstances should a gigolo be willing to support a woman. The woman insists on maintaining the one-up position; any sign of independence on the part of the gigolo is perceived as a threat. Her power is money and possibly status, the power of the parent over the child. His power over her resembles children's manipulation of their parents. They pout, sulk, withhold their presence, love, and affection until they get what they want. The relationship between the gigolo and his mistress is rigidly complementary and has the usual attendant power struggle.

Although the relationship between a gigolo and his mistress is businesslike and well defined, certain elements of society are outraged by the idea. And well they might be. This kind of relationship reflects a reversal of the conventional power exchange between men and women. "He's just using her," someone says in disgust. "But," says a timid voice, "isn't she using him as well?" The key word here is *use*. Perhaps a better one is *exploit*. As marriage counselors we see that all couples "use" one another: that is, they exchange benefits. We propose that exploitation occurs when either member of a couple contributes something to the relationship that he or she does not really want to give. For example, if a woman is resentful about her husband's not working and continues to support him even when he won't take a job, she is being exploited. She is allowing herself to be used.

Mutual agreement by a couple on a course of action differentiates exploitation from an exchange of benefits. When two people decide together on who takes what role or task for any period of time, they have freely negotiated an agreement. The ability to negotiate usually involves a great deal of role flexibility, which distinguishes the couples we've interviewed from the "kept man" couple. Only two of the older woman/ younger man pairs we have met have a negotiated agreement that is a reversal of a conventional marriage style.

Laura is a forty-four-year-old physiotherapist; Bruce is a sculptor. He is nine years younger than his wife. They have been married for ten years. When they married they made the decision that Bruce would devote himself to his work as a sculptor on a full-time basis. Laura earns most of the money that supports the household. In exchange, Bruce does some of the housework, chauffeurs the children to school and appointments. Bruce told us, "I'm sure there are men who would be suffering a lot of guilt because their wives were going out to work. I'd much rather she'd be home and have fun and could work when she wanted to, but I don't feel guilty about our decision." Laura added, "Look, I like working and I would work anyway. But Bruce is starting to get some commissions and we hope that after a while he'll be able to make enough for me to think about making a career transition of my own." At the moment Bruce and Laura's arrangement seems to satisfy them.

Most men, including younger men, would probably not make the decision Bruce did. Not only would they feel guilty about being supported by a woman, but they would have a very rough time holding onto their basic self-esteem. No matter how often someone says, "It's not what you earn, it's the kind of person you are that counts," we are all aware that in most cultures power often derives from the respect that is given to people who have more money than others.

And how about women? How might a woman feel about being the only financial support of the household? Only a rare few would consider it.

Almost all of the women we have spoken to would be absolutely unwilling to support their mates financially on a permanent basis. However, a number of women have told us that they would be willing to offer the younger man financial support on a temporary basis; that is, they expect him to assume his share of the financial burden as soon as he is able. Even with this kind of goodwill, women with younger mates who have less income and fewer savings than they do feel mild to acute discomfort with the situation.

The reason is not hard to find. Generally a woman has a background of being financially taken care of, first by her parents and then by her husband. The patterns of her conditioning have led her to believe that the proper behavior for a woman is to give up her ability to make money and to provide supportive services for a man in exchange for financial security. This, in turn, leads her to think of the services she renders her husband as a method of earning her sustenance. Since she has traded in her own earning ability as a part of her marriage contract, she equates the degree of love her husband feels for her with the amount of money he is willing to make and share with her. An older woman in a relationship with a younger man who doesn't have as much money as she has will often have a feeling that she is not really being taken care of: that is, he does not love and value her.

For a woman to take full responsibility for her own financial support and not expect it from anyone else is a new and often difficult experience. To share expenses with a man instead of expecting him to have more than she does is yet another step into a previously unexplored area. There are a lot of leftover feelings that have to be sorted out when a woman embarks on a relationship with a man who has less money than she does, even if the man is her own age or older.

Forty-seven-year-old executive Tina Carey commented on this new experience. Although she started working early in her life to help support herself, she always had a parent or a husband who had more money than she made and was willing to help her out. This is the first time in her life she's been completely financially responsible for herself. She's still experiencing the shrinking of her budget since she and her last husband separated. Tina said, "Thrift is built into me; I thought I'd planned for everything and would have money left over I could save. Now I find I'm just making it. When I was married I always had enough money to buy anything I wanted to; I can't now."

Tina has had for over two years a relationship with David, eleven years younger. He has a good income, but it is not equivalent to Tina's. They usually split costs or take turns paying for things. If they do something expensive, Tina pays for her share. Often she has ambivalent feelings about this arrangement. "I would love to be taken out all the time, have somebody pay for me. If someone offered to do that I would be quite entranced. I suppose anybody would be."

We asked Tina how she would feel if some man did, indeed, pick up all her expenses. Wouldn't she feel that she was, in some way, controlled by the person with more money? "No" — she shrugged — "as long as I have my own money I feel I'm in control because I can opt out."

Although Tina makes an excellent living, a part of her still yearns for an extended financial umbrella. However, Tina has made an important point. Even if she were eventually to involve herself with a man who was willing to take care of her financially, ultimately she remains autonomous, because she has an income sufficient for her own needs. We propose that this is the same situation that occurs when a man is married to an older woman who has more money than he. Although his income may be smaller, he is self-supporting. The woman may choose to share her income with the man, but he is not dependent on it. If he doesn't care for the situation, he can leave it.

Tina Carey's feeling of being let down when David does not offer to pay for both of them was reflected by several of the women we spoke to. They expressed concern about feeling devalued. Somewhat ruefully they admitted that they liked the idea of that extra financial support. But other women told us that even though they might not have as much spending money as women with wealthier mates, they would probably never again choose to be in such a dependent position.

To understand how a woman could reject the idea of being married to a man with more money, let us digress a bit and look at the changes in women's economic status over the last forty years.

The place of women in the American economy has altered considerably since the middle of the twentieth century. Today the economy demands the inclusion of women in the labor force. As a result, the working status of women is permanently changed. The family budget often requires two salaries. However, women workers are traditionally held responsible for housekeeping duties, care of children, and entertaining as well as their full-time jobs. The result is that a lot of working women find they have ended up with two full-time jobs. And many of them resent it.

Nevertheless, more and more women are committed to working as a way of life. They work to supplement family income or, if they are single, they work to support themselves. A divorced woman often must enter or rejoin the working force. Currently, many women are trained or educated for a specific kind of work and have a career goal in mind. But the chief by-product of being paid for her labor is that a working woman achieves a sense of economic independence and begins to question her previous subservient role. As a woman gains confidence and competence through working, she wants more decision-making power in regard to the family finances and more recognition for her accomplishments.

For an older woman, taking the step toward complete financial independence is satisfying in one way and frightening in another. She may enjoy feeling like a grownup instead of a child, knowing that she has the unquestioned right to do as she pleases with her money. But for several of the women we interviewed, a sense of personal and financial autonomy has been achieved only by grim determination and a constant struggle with self-doubt. A person who goes through this process usually is a member of a generation of women who were not encouraged toward monetary self-sufficiency. The financial independence that she creates for herself is hard won and she will not give it up easily. Her newly discovered sense of herself as having paid her dues to become a card-carrying member of the human race is still fragile.

The only power and prestige that some of these women have previously experienced in the world has been derived from their husbands' status. Often they are defining, for the first time, what they want from their lives. Although many of the women in older woman/younger man relationships have some money or property through divorce settlements, as well as worthwhile jobs, they are still in the process of finding their own places in life. In spite of many trappings of external success, a house, friends, and a job, they often don't feel like women of the world. They are still searching for their own significance in the scheme of things, and their idea of what constitutes position in the world may or may not be what the world considers important.

Nevertheless, certain women feel that the search for themselves can best be facilitated by securing a sound and independent financial base.

After her divorce, author and teacher Susan Howard, now forty-six, was wary of risking a new relationship. She was afraid that she might inadvertently slip back into earlier patterns of behavior and lose the sense of emotional and financial autonomy she had so painfully acquired. Susan looks back to where she was five years ago, when she met art therapist Peter Levin, then twenty-six: "I know now that one of the reasons I chose Peter was that he didn't have as much money as I did. My ex-husband is a wealthy and successful man, who left me to marry another woman. At that time I guess I equated success and money with rejection."

Susan explained how her living arrangement with Peter works. They pool their money for household and entertainment expenses. Each one puts in a percentage of his or her income. Right now, Peter's income is one-third of Susan's earnings. So Susan contributes two-thirds of their household account and Peter puts in one-third. It is important to Susan that Peter make his own living and cover his expenses, but she doesn't mind sharing her home and subsidizing Peter when they travel. In the last year, Peter's income has been going steadily upward. Susan is pleased about it. She would like to be able to share living expenses half and half. But she is adamant about going beyond that line again.

"I know that Peter is going to be very successful in his profession. He'll probably make a lot of money. Right now I can't see myself wanting any of it. In fact, I distrust it. I want to continue earning money through my own abilities. I want to buy my own necessities and my own luxuries. I hope I am never again in a position where I depend on anybody else for money."

Later, Susan did admit that her attitude might change. One of the things that she has discovered about herself is that she has no resentment about supporting another person for a limited period of time. "Every once in a while," she said cheerfully, "I think that maybe later on I'll take a break and let Peter support me. But then" — Susan shuddered — "it makes me go cold at the gut just thinking about it."

Susan's attitude is unusual. More commonly, older women

involved with younger men feel anxiety about having more money than their men. Liz Stefano, who is now thirty-eight, was still doing graduate work when she met and married Paul Stefano, now twenty-eight. During her last year of graduate school and her internship, Liz earned some money, but Paul contributed most of the household support. Now Liz is in private practice as a psychologist and doing well. Paul is proud and delighted and brags about his wife's financial potential.

Liz confided in us, "Every time Paul raves about how much money I'm going to make I get nervous. I fantasize him giving up his job and gleefully spending every cent I have. I know that he won't do any such thing, but a part of me still believes that men are supposed to make more money than women."

Liz is comforted by the fact that Paul has supported her for the last three years, but uneasy that her husband is content that she should make more money than he does.

Since the issue of a woman's having more money than her man is so directly contradictory to the conventional ideas of power in male/female relationships, we were not surprised that most women whose mates had less income were disturbed by that fact. They worried about their self-esteem, fearful that they might feel devalued if they supplied a larger share of income to the household. In general, the younger men were also uncomfortable about their relatively lower financial positions. The men had feelings of frustration and definite concerns about self-esteem, mostly to do with what other men might think of them. Often couples perceived the situation as socially embarrassing. Nevertheless, in most of the relationships where the woman had more money than the man, the couple were cooperatively working out the process of how they were going to earn and spend their combined incomes.

For one couple, however, the issue of the woman's having

more money has become a serious problem. The way money is valued and handled in any relationship is a crucial issue. As family therapists we often investigate the money issues in a relationship, not only to help reorganize the family's money transactions, but to discover important clues about what caused the relationship to break down.

Jennifer Selby, thirty-four, and Neil Saunders, twenty-five, are a couple whose relationship is disintegrating because of money problems. Jennifer makes an excellent living as a market analyst. For her, this is the latest of a series of career successes. Jennifer was orphaned at seventeen and has been supporting herself ever since. She was raised to believe that people should work hard and support themselves. She told us, "I would rather scrub floors than take a penny from anyone else." She has followed that ethic, worked hard, and put herself through college, earning her doctoral degree while working full-time. In addition, she has saved her money and invested those savings carefully against future need.

For the last five years Jennifer has lived with Neil Saunders. Neil comes from a comfortably well-to-do family. His parents have subsidized their children through their respective educations and Neil continues to receive a small allowance from them. Neil has completed law school and is preparing to take bar exams. During the time that he and Jennifer have lived together, he has had part-time jobs, often working as a bartender, jobs in which, according to Jennifer, he made very good money. In addition, he takes on most of the domestic chores that Jennifer detests and has been extremely supportive about her professional goals.

However, the relationship is in serious trouble. Jennifer is very unhappy that Neil is not working up to his potential. She feels that she has been the major financial support for the relationship since its beginning and she is deeply resentful. In addition, Jennifer is extremely ambitious for both herself and Neil. His relaxed attitude about life and work is very disturbing to her; she is terribly anxious about his reluctance to take work as seriously as she does. Jennifer loves Neil very much. She is grateful for the kind of support and caring he has given her, but it is not enough to make her happy. Her feelings about Neil at this time are very ambivalent.

"I feel guilty because Neil was very supportive during those painful years when I was getting my doctoral degree. In addition to the household chores, he helped me with the writing and research. I don't want to be one of those people where one spouse helped the other through law school or med school and then the spouse with the degree goes off to greener pastures. But Neil's got to make it for himself; I can't make it for him. I can't make him successful. And success I define so simply: if he just had a job."

In talking to Jennifer we discovered that she had never told Neil what she was thinking or feeling about this problem. She had occasionally hinted, but never clearly stated what was bothering her. She has attempted to resolve the issue by going to a city three thousand miles away on the pretext that she needed to travel in order to get the material for a book she is working on. Neil continues to live in the house that they shared for five years, and Jennifer continues to pay the rent on it. She is still in the same dilemma, but without the comfort and support of Neil's physical presence. And yet, Jennifer expects Neil to figure out somehow what is wrong without her letting him know exactly what she is thinking and feeling. The odds are that it won't happen.

When we asked Jennifer how they handled their mutual financial obligations, she told us that household bills were shared half and half and personal expenses were taken care of individually, but that since she made more money, she paid for the treats most of the time. Treats to Jennifer are movies, restaurants, a good bottle of wine, or gourmet food items. She also mentioned that when Neil was working he was extremely generous to her with whatever income he had. What she is angry about is Neil's reluctance to involve himself in money-making work, which is an important personal value to Jennifer. Jennifer is terribly afraid that this state of affairs is not merely a stage, but that Neil will never be willing to support himself in the way that Jennifer would prefer. She explained that she has no objection to supporting someone if that person can't work — because of illness, age, or handicap — for she has been partially supporting her grandmother for the last few years.

We propose that Jennifer and Neil's difficulties are only partially based on a money issue. Primarily, their conflict is caused by a severe communications problem and, secondarily, by a marked difference in values and attitudes about money: how, when, and how much of it is made, plus how and when and how much of it is spent. The first step toward clearing up these difficulties is discussing the problem. Jennifer needs to tell Neil what she expects of him and to find out what he is willing to do about it. There is a distinct possibility that if Neil knew how important this is to Jennifer and to the relationship, he would do what she is asking. Everything else in the relationship reflects great goodwill between the pair. If Neil says no, then Jennifer at least knows where she stands, and can make decisions accordingly without having to stay three thousand miles away.

But Jennifer told us, "We don't talk about this very much; I feel if he really loved me, it would be obvious." As long as Jennifer is not willing to tell Neil what she wants from him and from the relationship, we can pretty well predict a painful ending to the relationship.

Basically, people work out living arrangements, including money transactions, by making agreements about who shall be responsible for what in the relationship. It is one of the major ways of allowing two different individuals to live together relatively peaceably. All human beings have agreements with each other about everything in their lives, whether they are consciously aware of it or not. For instance, in a healthy traditional marriage, the husband and wife both agree on their respective tasks and roles. He may work; she may tend the house and children; but everybody has agreed to perform certain tasks and is willing to deliver what they have promised. When promises are kept, trust grows and the relationship can become a protective bulwark against the chaos of life instead of a major war zone. Family therapists refer to these agreements as contracts.

Stan Kaplan, Gestalt and family therapist, tells his clients to put a sign above their beds saying, "No contract; no contact!"

Contracts are not based on love. People can love each other but not necessarily be able to live together. Those of us who have experienced divorce can vouch for that. Contracts are actually based on a feeling of goodwill, the desire to give the other person the benefit of the doubt until he or she proves incapable of being trusted with it. Conscious working out of contracts is essential to the continued good health of a relationship. People who are unaware of the contracts they have made with each other often get into conflict.

For instance, Jennifer has an unspoken contract with Neil regarding their financial arrangements. Until one of them voices dissatisfaction with their present contract, nothing will change. Contracts preserve the autonomy of each person in the relationship. They are openly requested and negotiated behavioral changes that eliminate most of the power struggle between a couple.

Contracts need to be based exclusively on behavioral changes instead of attitude changes. Let us demonstrate. Fold your hands together. Look and see which thumb you have on top, right or left. Put the other thumb on top without moving your fingers. How does it feel? Strange? Uncomfortable? Do you feel a little anxiety? You have folded your hands together in the same way, with the same thumb on top, all of your life. This is called a habit, or a behavior. When you shift the position of your thumb you are changing a tiny, but deeply ingrained, bit of behavior. However, if you were asked to keep your thumbs in the new position for a period of time, you would have complete control over the operation. From this exercise you can learn three important parts of making a behavior change. One, a behavior change is anything that you have *conscious, physical control* over; two, it will feel uncomfortable for a while; and three, if you are willing to do it, after a time the discomfort will disappear and you will have a new habit or behavior.

On the other hand, when someone says to another person, "You've really got to change that attitude," the speaker can't expect much in the way of change. An attitude is derived from a person's whole experience of life, his or her childhood, environmental conditioning, religion, philosophy, and everything that has ever happened to that person. Attitude comes from our whole perceptual model of the world. Each human being's attitude about life is subtly different from every other one's, no matter how similar they seem. You can't negotiate with someone to change his or her personality. You can only change partners. But you can negotiate with someone to change his or her behavior. When people have a solidly working relationship, whether it be traditional or avant-garde, they are constantly, if sometimes not totally consciously, requesting changes of behavior, negotiating agreements, and mutually exchanging benefits.

In an older woman/younger man relationship, an understanding of contractual systems is essential to working out the handling of money, particularly where the couple is concerned about the woman's having more money. Some of these couples have a traditional arrangement, in which the man earns all or most of the money. This is a contractual system that is familiar, and most of us know the guidelines. But if the pair have similar incomes or the woman has more money than the man, there are no familiar models. Openly negotiated agreements are essential to making this kind of system work.

A number of the couples we've interviewed who had similar incomes have had few money conflicts. Often they share on a his, hers, and theirs basis. Both contribute equally to a mutual household account, and a certain amount is reserved for the exclusive personal use of each partner.

A few of the couples we've talked to have told us about periods of having relatively no money at all. The problem then wasn't sharing; it was not having any money to share. The Courtney-Feins confided in us that they had prided themselves on having no conflicts about money until they began to earn substantial amounts. Then their divergent value systems began to appear. After years of sharing one broken-down vintage Pontiac they had to make some major adjustments about the use of money. The result is that Barbara has acquired a brand-new Seville and Jeff is the proud possessor of a pickup truck. Success symbols are definitely different things to each of them.

Sometimes, no money at all can be a blessing to an older woman/younger man relationship. Simone Hartley, forty-four, never had to worry that Robert Foulon, twenty, was interested in her for her money. "From some eighteen years of marriage to an Englishman, I had very set ideas on how one should live, on what was essential to living. Suddenly, I was separated from my husband, I was in debt to my ears, and I hadn't a sou. I had no money; Robert had no money. So fair enough, I might have shared cornflakes and eggs with him, but he used his free tickets as a photo-journalist for us to go to the theatre and concerts together, so that, in a way, he was taking me out. He certainly didn't have the money to buy them. But he did have the odd bit of money coming in from his work, too, and he would go and buy food for us." Simone chuckled. "No, he definitely was not there for the money. There simply wasn't any."

Amy Carson, aged fifty, is another woman who finds the idea that a younger man might want her for her money very amusing. Amy was married for many years to a man who was a compulsive gambler. Her way of dealing with the situation was to never acquire anything in the way of money or valuables that he could gamble away. For twenty-five years she has lived frugally but pleasantly in the same rent-controlled apartment on Manhattan's upper West Side. But other elements of Amy's life have changed. Presently she is a well-paid textile designer, although she is considering leaving her job to go back to being a full-time artist, a move she has made from time to time over the years. "I'll free-lance enough as a designer to pay the rent and food and an occasional trip. That's all I need. To me it's like a game. I never feel poor."

Amy lives with Mark Linden, thirty-eight. Amy and Mark met many years ago, when both were married to their previous spouses. They were employed by the same firm, and the two couples became friends. Several years after the breakup of their respective marriages, they ran into each other and a romance ensued. Mark had left the textile business to teach full-time in a community college. Then he took a leave of absence to write a book. When the book was finished, his teaching job was no longer available. Since then he has taught part-time, worked as a machinist, and, recently, he took over a full-time job as Amy's assistant designer, when her previous assistant suddenly quit and Amy was left in the lurch with a big job to finish. But Mark is really set on getting another teaching job. Until that time, however, Mark's income is considerably less than Amy's.

Sitting in Amy and Mark's living room having coffee is something like being inside a menagerie at feeding time. Cats and more cats, in every size, shape, and color, are all over the place. They are curled up on laps, chairs, and tables; one is draped over the mantelpiece. A very little one drifts in from the kitchen to have its ears scratched, and Amy explains that the cats are all hers. "There's one more," Amy says, "but he's probably hiding under a bed someplace because he's too shy to come out."

Mark turns to us. "You asked us how we divide up our household expenses. We split everything fifty-fifty, except for the cat food and the liquor."

"You see," Amy explained, "there are so many of them, cats and friends. I don't think it's fair for Mark to pay for cat food. And neither he nor I drink much, but I have a few friends who consume inordinate quantities."

Vacations are handled by Mark's putting up whatever he has and Amy's paying the rest. We asked if that was okay with them. "I'm not crazy about it," Mark said, "but if we didn't do it that way we couldn't take the trip together, and Amy, right now, is so far ahead of me financially that it is no problem for her."

Amy told us that she would like to be even more generous but she still has feelings of distrust about money from her first marriage. By the time she had received her ex-husband's half of the January rent, it was June. But even though Mark may have less money than her previous husband, his sense of financial responsibility to the relationship is very different.

If Amy wants to go out to supper more times per week than Mark can afford, she has to foot the bill. And in some situations, Mark will pay her way. For instance, one day Amy wasn't feeling well, and took a cab to her office for an important meeting, which was then canceled. Still not feeling well, and being frustrated, she was lamenting that she would have to pay another five dollars to take a cab home. "Paying ten dollars to go to and from work when you're there for fifteen minutes annoys me," said Amy. Mark gave her three out of the second five dollars to get her over the hurdle.

We asked Mark and Amy if they had any feelings about Amy's being able to buy whatever she wanted while Mark was on a tight budget. Amy told us that she sometimes does feel guilty about buying something when Mark can't. When buying Indian jewelry on a trip to the Southwest, she had the feeling she should buy him something because she had bought herself something. Mark didn't agree. "First of all," he said, "I like those things, but they aren't as important to me as going down to Canal Street to buy electronic equipment. And I do that anyway. Even if I had the money, I probably wouldn't buy the same stuff Amy does."

They agreed that the only issue they have difficulty discussing, as a result of their different incomes, is that Amy wants to buy a house in the country and Mark doesn't get excited by the idea, since he is not in a position to involve himself financially with a house.

Amy and Mark have developed a workable system of money handling. In our experience as family therapists, we know that money can be one of the major problem areas in a relationship. The problem can sometimes stem from the fact that there is not enough of it, but more often the struggle comes from having no acknowledged agreement about the sharing or spending of what money is available.

When we discussed money negotiations with Mark and Amy, Amy remarked that her goodwill towards Mark about money was probably based on the ten years of trusted friendship before they became lovers. Mark agreed that the long-term friendship was a major part of their relationship.

Mark talked about his income's going up in the near future. At that time he would want Amy to resign her job and start painting again. Amy has had to be financially self-sufficient all of her adult life. How would she feel about Mark's being the major financial support? Amy pondered the question. "I wouldn't like feeling like a parasite, being dependent financially, and yet from time to time I notice this built-in mechanism that says, 'The man is supposed to take care of you.' Right now, it's a moot question." Mark concluded, "As long as I'm not making any great amount of money, Amy is very reluctant to give up her high-level salary."

In Mark and Amy's relationship, each is a valued person. What work Amy chooses is as important as any work decision Mark might make. There is give-and-take and sharing, both of which are particularly important in a relationship where one person has less money than the other. Each person sets a realistic limit on what he or she can give without feeling deprived. Feelings about money and the use of it are openly discussed, argued about, and eventually an agreement is negotiated.

The flow of Amy and Mark's relationship is based on a conscious acceptance of differences. Amy hates the subway; Mark can't stand buses. When they come home from work, each uses a different form of transportation. Mark picks up a few groceries, waits for Amy at the corner of their block, and they walk home together.

There are problems that arise in the older woman/younger man relationship that may seem to be connected with money, but the money aspect itself is mostly symbolic. This kind of problem is certainly not typical of the older woman/younger man relationship and hardly exclusive to it. One major source of money conflict between any couple, including older woman/younger man couples, is that each partner may have a different value system concerning money. An individual value system would include how much money a person is supposed to make, and how that money should be used.

Janis, forty-five, comes from a hardworking family whose members are extremely careful in their use of money. If you bought new shoes, they were to be kept in the closet until some big occasion came along. Janis lives with Jim, thirty-five. In Jim's family, too, people worked hard, but the money they earned was easy come, easy go. Jim will buy a very expensive pair of moccasins and wear them to his factory the next day. Janis goes up the wall. To her this is not only wasteful; it is practically degenerate. Jim, on the other hand, can be very irritated with Janis because she won't buy fine crystal to enhance an extraordinary wine. To her, the wine tastes just as good out of a jelly glass. Differences in value systems don't always break up a relationship, but they can generate conflict and make the relationship unpleasant.

Generally, if people accept each other's differences, they can work out money systems by having his, hers, and their bank accounts. The third bank account is for paying normal household expenses. That means that only major purchases and vacations have to be negotiated. Other books have dealt more extensively with money negotiations in connection with individual value systems; we mention them here only to point out that this kind of problem is typical of all relationships.

One of our interviewees told us that her younger boyfriend is openhanded about money while she is rather tight with it. Nevertheless, when they go somewhere, he never seems to have any money with him. She generally ends up paying. Then she has to remember the amount and remind him of it, at which time he repays her. She finds the whole thing extremely annoying. This is a money behavior that is not confined to older woman/younger man relationships.

Basically, this woman has an accurate perception of her boyfriend's attitude about money. He is simply not as concerned with money as she is. He would also like to have someone else take the responsibility for handling it so that he doesn't have to worry about it. And whether she likes it or not, that is exactly what this woman has been maneuvered into doing. Being forgetful about money is a behavior that is often annoying to other people. The best way to deal with another's upsetting behavior is to request a specific change, saying something like, "Please plan to have money in your pocket when we go out. I don't like to take responsibility for always having money."

An issue that is often connected with money is the question of status. Since we have already talked about social status in Chapter 3, we'll concern ourselves here with career status. Generally, if the woman has more money, she is apt to be farther ahead in her career than the younger man is. There are definitely emotional and social implications to this position which can place additional stress on the older woman/younger man relationship. If he feels that he is supposed to be more important than the woman, the younger man may feel a loss of self-esteem; he may even feel envious and insignificant. If he is extremely competitive, he will feel these things acutely.

In turn, most women are afraid of achieving more than their men; they are afraid of being considered masculine or of losing their desirability, which is their major asset if they are beyond childbearing age.

Most dynamic women seek men who are more accomplished than themselves, in order to avoid even appearing to be more capable than the men. By carefully staying just below the scope of the men's achievements, they can actualize at least part of their potential and remain feminine in society's eyes.

One of the most difficult parts of the older woman/younger man relationship is coming to terms with these concepts. Many such relationships have foundered because one or both partners were not willing to let go of preconceived ideas about masculinity and femininity. It takes a singularly self-confident woman and an equally self-confident man to override these highly conditioned reflexes.

After seven years together, Sean, thirty, separated from his wife, Claire, thirty-eight. Both had started new business careers two years earlier, but Claire had achieved remarkable success in a very short time, while Sean's business was just beginning to take off. Sean admits that his wife's accomplishment probably had more to do with her being older and more experienced than he, than her having any more innate brains or talent. Still, he found the situation very frustrating. There was always the possibility that Claire might have more ability, and his highly competitive nature couldn't tolerate that. Although there were other problems, the threat of perpetually living in the shadow of Claire's success was one major factor in ending Sean and Claire's marriage.

Amy Carson, fifty, talked about her reluctance to give up her high-salaried job to go back to painting. "Actually," she said, "it's not the money. If I were guaranteed the same attention, the publicity, the interviews, the feeling of being up there, for my paintings, I wouldn't even care about the money." Mark told us that when he first met Amy, he knew Amy the artist. Although he is pleased by Amy's success, he's not sure that the prestigious designer is the real Amy. The first thing he did when he moved in with her was get her neglected studio back into shape.

Does Mark have ambiguous feelings about Amy's success?

He freely admits it. He is concerned that she is a designer at the expense of being an artist. Might he also be jealous and a little intimidated? Maybe. But whatever Amy chooses, it will be her decision, and Mark is quite capable of living with it.

When Kelly, now thirty-nine, met Seth, who is thirty-one, eight years ago, Seth was a struggling musician. Today Seth is a criminal attorney just beginning his practice, while Kelly is an executive with a major studio. Kelly has an established position in a high-powered world. And even though Seth is a functioning professional, he may decide to be a public defender, rather than have a lucrative private practice. Kelly has had thoughts of taking time off and writing a book, but, as Seth points out, they both like to live well. Seth and Kelly have a number of decisions to make. Would Kelly be willing to give up the status she now has and the considerable income that goes with it? Would Seth be willing to alter his career direction to generate the money that would ensure their lifestyle while Kelly writes her book? Seth is a very high-powered person himself. Can he accept the idea that Kelly will always be the major money-maker in the relationship and that her social prestige will be greater than his?

The alternatives that Kelly and Seth must consider for their future are an example of both the difficulties and the richness of many older woman/younger man relationships. These relationships create an unusual number of options for living, but only if the initial difficulties inherent in the situation are resolved.

When the woman in an older woman/younger man relationship has more money and, possibly, status than the man, the couple can choose to be discouraged because contemporary conventions find their relationship unpalatable, or they can use their unusual situation to help them both evolve, personally and professionally.

Without question the younger man may find it initially difficult to maintain his self-esteem because he is not the major source of income for his household, but he may discover that what he gains, instead, are opportunities for redirecting and expanding his life that very rarely occur in marriages where the man's income is the essential one. And although there are very real social and emotional complications for the relationship, the option for both partners to share, change, and grow can more than compensate for any adjustment that needs to be made.

9 ·

SEX

THE CLASSIC VIEW OF AN OLDER WOMAN/YOUNGER man relationship is that it exists primarily for sexual gratification. It is not difficult to understand why. In the European cultures, it has been customary for centuries for sexually experienced older women to initiate young men into the mysteries and pleasures of sex. A discreet affair between an older woman and a younger man is also acceptable, provided that it is brief and in no way intrudes on the more serious business of their lives.

In literature and film, the older woman has been stereotyped as a sophisticated seductress, luring the young innocent into her honeyed arms to partake of delights he has never known before. And the man, in turn, possesses the overheated blood of youth, which will quicken the desire and rejuvenate the fading vitality of the aging woman. Traditionally, then, the pervading image of an older woman/younger man relationship consists of a series of highly erotic encounters.

Is there any reality to other people's fantasies about the sex life of the older woman/younger man couple? And, when these alliances are not intended to be brief affairs, can such intense sexuality sustain itself through the kinds of stress that these couples will face in a long-term committed relationship?

Our older women and younger men interviewees admit that they do make a first-rate sexual combination under good conditions. They are not superstuds or tigers, but they are unusually active sexually. Many couples describe an electrifying first meeting and they speak glowingly about their sex lives. Without question, they place a high priority on sex.

The people we have interviewed experienced a variety of initial sexual responses to each other. The men, for instance, talked about feeling very shy when approaching an older woman sexually because she might think their interest ridiculous. Women have confided that they were equally reserved about being seductive for fear of being thought dirty old ladies. Women were also concerned about obvious signs of physical aging in themselves which made them feel particularly vulnerable about making love with a younger man. About half the people we interviewed made love early in the relationship, just as most people of equal age do as a result of contemporary acceptance of almost immediate sexual contact.

The other half of our interviewees had a different kind of story to tell. What they describe sounds more like an old-fashioned courtship period. It's not that these couples didn't feel an immediate sexual attraction, but social taboos surrounding the older woman/younger man relationship made them very careful in approaching each other sexually. Often the relationship started as a friendship. Most of these couples were aware that they had sexual feelings for each other from their first meeting, but considered them inappropriate to the relationship and did not immediately express them. After weeks or even months of a developing friendship, mutual trust enabled these couples to begin a sexual relationship.

We asked our interviewees to tell us specifically what they

liked about their sexual relationships. The women told us that what they liked most was that younger men are more likely to accept and encourage their newly developed sexuality. To explain the differences, they often contrasted the sexual behavior of younger men with that of contemporaries or men who were older.

A forty-one-year-old businesswoman talked about her sexual relationship with her thirty-year-old husband. She said he encourages her to do whatever she wishes while making love. She plays different roles: gentle lover, firm aggressor, uninhibited playmate. In her thirties, when she was single, she dated men of varying ages. Older men were put off by her sexual assertiveness. They fought for control or they stayed away from her. "There I was," she sighed, "finally freed from my sexual inhibitions and it wasn't appreciated. In fact, it was a strike against me."

Male contemporaries oftentimes do not like to know that their partners have had previous sexual experience. A psychologist we interviewed told us wryly, "Each time I start a relationship with a man my own age, I grow a new hymen. Somehow they seem to want me, a twice-married woman, forty-five years old, to pretend to an innocence I don't have." But a woman who tells a man what she likes or initiates sexual moves is obviously experienced. The male contemporary may perceive the sexually experienced woman as slightly shopworn, while the younger man tends to experience her evolving libido as the most wonderful thing that ever happened to him.

In addition, older women told us that they prefer sex with younger men because the younger men enjoy the whole experience of sex. Many older women complain that male contemporaries tend to emphasize sexual performance rather than sensual pleasure. A forty-five-year-old teacher said that she had noticed a sense of desperation in lovemaking with men her own age. "It's almost as if they have to prove something to themselves and to me. And men older than I — they're proud of what they produce. It's like they're saying, 'See that? Two orgasms in a row' or 'Wow! I just did it for four hours straight.' "

Of her experience with lovers her own age, Susan Howard, forty-six, said, "I really got sick of being criticized and evaluated sexually. The topper was a psychologist who told me I was anorgasmic because I didn't have an orgasm the first time I slept with him. Younger men don't worry so much about performance, mine or theirs. They seem able to enjoy the warmth, the closeness, and the sexual contact without excessive pressure to make it perfect."

In differentiating sex as an experience from sex as a performance, the emphasis is on whatever actually happens in a single sexual encounter. There are no rules. Whatever pleasure both partners feel is the experience. This emphasis requires an awareness of feelings and a desire to communicate them. So any given sexual encounter may be brief, long-lasting, stopped before orgasm, limited to snuggling, making out, or a sensual massage. It may be serious, aggressive, melancholy, or silly. Since men are traditionally trained not to feel, they tend to focus instead on performance with orgasm as a goal. Since they judge themselves by their sexual performance, they are loath to let go of the duration between erection and orgasm as the be-all and end-all of sex.

Psychologist Herb Goldberg urges men to allow themselves to enjoy their emotions. In his book *The Hazards of Being Male,* he discusses contemporary male sexuality: "The beginnings of a new male consciousness in the area of sexuality will require, along with being fully aware of his feelings, a different way of interpreting his responses. It will demand an awareness of the constant, countless, subtle ways he has allowed himself to become conditioned into accepting the burden of sexual performance. . . . The preoccupation with techniques commonly seen today usually signals an underlying awareness of the death of passion and spontaneity. . . . The emphasis on the facts of physiology may be interesting and intellectually enlightening but has nothing to do with the experience of sex itself."[1]

Goldberg believes stereotypic role behavior is a trap. It is impossible to be a strong, silent, male and spontaneous at the same time. When a man frees himself from the traditional male role he can allow himself a wide variety of sexual behaviors. Many of the young men we interviewed have chosen to become open, feeling people. Some have changed because they were radicalized by the social and political ferment of the sixties and seventies. Many have been deeply affected by the woman's liberation movement. A few are emulating unusually tender fathers. A few are in rebellion against distant, restrained fathers or families. Whatever the cause, they bring their emotions into lovemaking. The older women experience their younger partners as spontaneous, tender, and passionate.

Linda, a forty-seven-year-old lawyer, eloquently describes her thirty-five-year-old lover's sexual passion. 'Frank drowns himself in sex. When he has had an orgasm and is coming out of it, the image that occurs to me is that he looks like someone crawling up out of the sea. I see him coming up from the depths, just pulling himself out of the ocean, just dripping. I have never known another person who was so totally surrendered in sex as he. The sexual image I have of Frank is one of my most tender memories. It is enormously moving. I think I would get charged up for the next time by just looking at him when we finished making love."

Linda met Frank in law school fourteen years ago. She was thirty-three, divorced after twelve years of marriage, and had two children. Frank was twenty-one and single. Their relationship began as a friendship. After several months, it developed into a love affair and continued for about eight years. Linda has since married a man who is her contemporary in age, while Frank has remained a very close friend. Their sexual relationship was extraordinary for each of them. Their experience was similar to the experience of at least twenty-five percent of our couples, particularly the couples who are at least a decade apart in age.

Couples with over ten years of age difference rarely expect anything but a friendship at the beginning. Many of these couples told us they hung around together for three to nine months before they confessed that they were sexually attracted to each other. The conditioning against such liaisons kept them from considering one another as legitimate sexual partners. Even when they realized they were attracted, each hesitated about making the first move for fear of looking foolish in the other's eyes.

Linda told us that her relationship with Frank fostered the growth of her self-esteem. Many of the older women we interviewed told us the same thing. Frank's enjoyment of Linda brought her to a high point of self-confidence. She explained that at the time when she and Frank started their relationship she began to be aware that she was a beautiful woman. She knew before the relationship started that she was a valuable woman. But with Frank, she felt that she was a competent lover and good to look at. "In no way did I feel as I had often felt as a younger woman, constantly questioning my physical desirability. Are my breasts all right because they hang a little? Maybe I'm a little fat in my belly? Thinking all those things that so many women bring into bed with them. When I was with Frank I felt at some kind of peak of female beauty."

Older women agree that the sexual attention of a good-looking young man is a big boost to their self-esteem. It comes as no surprise that older women very much enjoy the physical attractiveness of their younger partners. And when someone you believe is attractive thinks you are, too, it is definitely enhancing to your ego.

Older women say they enjoy sex with younger men because they feel a safe acceptance, which allows them the freedom to take over sometimes in lovemaking, to experiment, and to express their feelings. A focus on the experience of sex with less attention to performance is what older women say they appreciate about younger men. Younger men are attentive and willing to be tender.

"What," we asked the younger men, "do you like about your sexual experience with older women? Is it really any different?" Several young men reminded us that sex was good basically because they were in love and because their friendships created a safe environment for lovemaking. Such factors are not age-related. They are often the necessary ingredients for satisfying lovemaking. Then the men went on to speak more specifically about what they liked sexually about older women.

Younger men say they find older women sexually exciting. But if older women have, in the past, represented flab, wrinkles, and sagging flesh, how is it that some younger men think older women are arousing? In part, the answer is that many older women don't look older. A woman over thirty today looks ten or even twenty years younger than her mother or grandmother did at the same age.

Appearances can be misleading. When we began interviewing for this book we theorized that some older women/ younger men couples, upon meeting each other, had assumed they were closer in age than they actually were. Since so many women these days look younger, and men can sometimes look a little older than their chronological age, we guessed that these couples might have originally miscalculated their age difference. In a number of cases this was true. One man, aged twenty-one, thought his older woman friend was in her late twenties when she was actually thirty-four. The woman thought, because of his behavior and beard, that the man was in his late twenties. An age difference of thirteen years seemed at first to be only about six years.

A thirty-five-year-old man described why he is sexually attracted to his forty-five-year-old wife: "It definitely has to do with my wife being older. I have always found that with younger women you're either teaching them or having bad sex. My wife is more liberated; she knows what she wants. She's more open in expressing what she wants sexually."

One man told us why he thinks older women are sexy in general: "I find older women sexier because they are freer, not freer in a libertine kind of a way, but simply freer about themselves. I don't sense from them a kind of push-pull about being sexual; they have incorporated their own sexuality. In some ways I find them much more sensual as people than younger women. Younger women may be more attractive and more appealing in appearance because they are more nubile, but I think older women are more languorous. They allow their bodies to flow more. They are more willing to be experimental in sex. They permit themselves a range of choices that younger women, either out of strong socialization or inhibition or ignorance, just are not interested in. I find that sexy."

Like the thirty-five-year-old man just quoted, Paul Stefano, twenty-eight, agrees that older women know their sexual needs better, are freer to talk about what they want. In addition, he is pleased that Liz shares the responsibilities in lovemaking. Paul says: "Older women are more responsive and comfortable with their sexuality. They say what they like; they know what they like. Often, when I have asked women my age to make love to me, they didn't really want to do it. They didn't want to take over. They didn't know what to do. I like to be made love to. I like to lie back and take it in. I like to be pursued."

A twenty-nine-year-old man told us he thought the difference between younger women and older women is that older women fully participate in making love. As he put it, "They don't just lie there." The older woman's responsiveness breeds more of the same in him. It is a sparking process that enhances the sexual experience.

While she may not have the gift of youth, the older woman does bring the richness of her maturity, her vitality, and the excitement of diversity to the relationship. It's like comparing fresh new wine to a fine aged vintage. Each has its place in the scheme of things. Benjamin Franklin, who was very much a man of the world, wrote, "Advice to a Younger Man" in 1745. This often-published letter lists eight reasons why a man should choose an older woman for himself. Franklin notes that the conversation of older women is more agreeable and knowledgeable. The letter states that sex with an older woman is at least equal to sex with a young woman and often superior, as practice leads to improvement. He ends the letter with the remark, "They are so grateful. . . ."[2]

It is possible to hear "They are so grateful" as condescending, yet gratitude and appreciation are close in meaning. Older women do appreciate younger men. The younger men seem to like being appreciated. It is very gratifying to be loved, to be valued, to be admired. And someone who feels appreciated usually appreciates in turn.

Another reason young men like going to bed with older women is because they don't have to work as hard to get them there. The man does not have to battle his way into the woman's bed; he has been invited. And once she is in bed, the older woman is relaxed and receptive. She is at ease with her body and her own sexuality. Being met halfway takes an enormous amount of pressure off the young man. The result is that the younger man, like the older woman, reports a rise in his sexual self-esteem.

Major studies on human sexual behavior have suggested

that older women and younger men are better matched sexually than same-age partners or couples in which the man is older. Biological research shows that women reach their peak of sexual functioning between their late twenties and early forties, and then maintain that level. A man's sexual drive supposedly peaks between his late teens and the age of twenty-five and then gradually begins to diminish. By mating with a younger man, the older woman is getting a man who is closer to his sexual peak than an older man would be.

But where does biology end and sociology begin? In our opinion, a woman's development into a sexually responsive adult has as much, if not more, to do with her social conditioning as her biology. Consider carefully that women in our society grow up with an entirely different message about sex from the one men are given. Men are tacitly encouraged from childhood to explore every sexual possibility. There is something not quite manly in male virginity. Pursuit, seduction, and sexual conquest of the female is for most men an almost obsessive preoccupation by early adolescence. Some of them never get over it.

Not so for the young female of our culture. She is told, directly or indirectly, from the beginning, that she must never appear to be sexually available. Furthermore, she is encouraged to resist her own sexual feelings, to regard her sexuality as something dangerous.

Although the young woman has developed feelings of sexual excitement, she is often successful in controlling her physiological responses to lovemaking. The possible pleasure she may feel in having sexual intercourse is nipped in the bud by guilt.

In addition to being trained to discourage sexual intimacy, she is held responsible for controlling any sexual behavior between herself and the boys she dates. Her psychosexual functioning is conditioned by such social messages as "Wait for marriage," or "Sexual women are promiscuous."

Like most girls of the fifties, Liz Stefano was taught that sex is reserved for marriage. She carefully observed the rules and, at twenty, married the first man she was sexually intimate with. She recalls her late teens: "So often my friends and I have laughed and made fun of our early sexual training. The image of us with our legs permanently crossed, never to be uncrossed, protecting our treasure. And when we got married, of course we didn't know how to use that treasure. It is a bizarre, pathetic picture. All that silly fear — and for what? So that we could spend the years between twenty and thirty trying to get free from all the caution, control, ignorance, and denial of our sexuality?"

The young women we see these days in our counseling practice are usually sexually active; however, they continue their mothers' pattern of sexual repression of response. They often do not fully enjoy sex; they are rarely orgasmic; they are unable to let go in sex and enjoy themselves. In addition, young women have a new pressure, one which their mothers did not have. Since we have passed through an era of sexual freedom and experimentation, new expectations have developed. Young women often expect themselves to be sexually expressive, uninhibited, and knowledgeable. As usual, underlying attitudes are slow to change. Thus, young women act as though they are sexually free while they feel as inhibited as their mothers did in their twenties.

In Western culture, however, most women go through considerable changes in their sexual behavior between thirty and forty. In many situations, married life provides an acceptable place for women's sexual responses to develop. By the time she is in her thirties, a woman is usually comfortable with her own sexuality, and for the first time she is feeling an awakening sexual responsiveness. She may have been sexually active from late adolescence, but being sexually functional and totally sexually responsive are two different things.

For many young married couples in our society, there is an imbalance of sexual responsiveness. The young husband is ready for passionate sexual involvement, while the young wife is mostly interested in cuddling. Her physical and emotional sexual development is retarded. The older woman, however, having shed her repressive conditioning, is now ready for the kind of intense sexual responsiveness that the young man experiences.

Susan Howard, forty-six, takes up the sexual development story where Liz leaves off: "It takes the woman a lot longer in our society to free herself, to take responsibility for her own sexuality and be comfortable with it. I remember, very specifically, being married about six years — I was about thirty-one years old — and all of a sudden being aware that all kinds of new things were going on in my body. I was feeling some responses that I never felt before. Sex had been okay but now there was something special happening. I remember checking this out with several other female friends of about the same age to say, 'Is this happening to you?' and everybody said, 'Yes, it is.' Somehow, for me, married sex was legitimate sex, so I could start feeling pleasure in it."

It is quite possible that the sexual compatability experienced in many older woman/younger man relationships is at least as much the result of social conditioning as it is the function of biology. The fact is that a younger man and an older woman are often at a similar level of sexual development. Physically and emotionally, they are equally capable of surrendering themselves to each other, allowing a deepening of the relationship on a sexual level that may not occur when the younger man has a sexual partner his own age. As sex is such a major part of most human relationships, equal sexual responsiveness is an important aspect of the attraction that older women and younger men feel for each other.

A sexually responsive woman is on her way to being a sexually assertive woman. She will make suggestions; she will ask for the kind of loving she needs. She is able to initiate lovemaking, even take the lead entirely. She may ask a man to tell her what pleases him.

Since most men in the older woman's generation have learned to be in charge of sex, it is often difficult for them to give up the lead or to tolerate a woman asking for what she wants. The behavior change is frightening for many men. Sex therapists are reporting an upsurge in impotence. According to a special report in *Newsweek* magazine, titled "How Men Are Changing," "The shift in male attitudes [toward the changes in women] has scarcely reached phenomenal proportions. It is apparent among younger educated men in their twenties and thirties, the group usually quickest to respond to new social currents. The majority of older men have barely modified their views of male-female roles."[3]

Young men begin their sexual experiences earlier than in previous times. They have grown up in a period of increasing sexual freedom, and, in addition, men in general are not taught to repress their sexuality; they are taught to express it. They do not have to hold back their desires. A man is allowed to sow his wild oats. He is never promiscuous, only a bit of a Don Juan. As we have mentioned before, both language and cultural training encourage a permissive attitude toward male sexuality. Thus, a very young man may be as sexually experienced as an older woman.

The added cultural ingredient in today's young man is that he is influenced by a reaction against his father's macho values. Paul Stefano, twenty-eight, doesn't want to accept the traditional male sexual role. He saw his father, as well as other men of his father's generation, take charge of all aspects of family life, including sex. He has decided it is not worth it. In addition, it does not suit him to be always in charge of lovemaking. He prefers that Liz share the responsibility.

Today's young man allows himself to be openly passive in sex, thus freeing himself from the burden of always being in charge. In a relationship with an older woman he does not have to be the initiator or take the teacher role all the time.

Both the older woman and the younger man make a valued contribution to their sexual experience. She contributes her sexual self-knowledge, her willingness to share responsibility, and her openness to sexual exploration. He contributes his appreciation, his acceptance of her sexual development. Both tend to have a relaxed, flexible, open attitude toward sex.

The biological and sociological matching of the older woman and the younger man sounds idyllic. It is exceptional, but nothing is idyllic forever. When the honeymoon period is over, in six months, in one year, or in two years, what happens to sexual attraction and consequently to their sex life? Over the long term these couples generally have the same problems as any other couple. They experience loss of interest in sex, disagreements over the frequency and the pace of sex, and the disruption of sex due to the birth of a child.

Carla, a thirty-eight-year-old banking executive, described a stormy sexual history with her husband, Joe, ten years younger. They have been married for seven years.

"We started out as a wildly sexual couple. From the time we began to make love we both seemed insatiable. We made love many times a week, often three times a day. We could hardly keep our hands off one another. I remember moments when I cried from joy and pleasure." Gradually, after eight or nine months, lovemaking became less frequent. At about the same time Carla began to notice things about the way Joe made love that she didn't like. They would argue about ways to kiss, timing of orgasm, how to touch. Joe was very offended by Carla's requests. She alternated feeling angry toward herself and toward him. Then Joe began to defend himself. He complained that Carla didn't make enough sounds during sex so he could know that she was responding. "At times the conflict would die down and sex was pleasant," Carla explained, "and then it would be as though he had forgotten our talks." To support her position Carla asked Joe to read up on sexual functioning, but he'd start the books and not finish them.

In the fifth year of their marriage Carla became pregnant. But she and Joe decided that they weren't really suited for the responsibility of having a child. Carla had an abortion. Although this sad event drew them together, for sometime afterward Carla's interest in sex dropped markedly. Joe felt rejected. Carla wondered how they would ever survive the problems in their sex life. Other parts of their relationship remained satisfying. They were good friends and companions. As Carla tells it, the good times together, the pleasant lifestyle they had built, and, most of all, their strong commitment to the marriage helped them pass through these periods of distress.

Carla goes on to describe her feelings: "So many times in the thick of the bad times I thought, 'What am I doing here? In this the kind of lovemaking I'm going to live with for the rest of my life? Can I live with it?' I guess I didn't leave because I don't think running away solves a problem. I kept hoping. I just couldn't believe such a bright man could ignore or not understand what I was saying. But recently Joe began to make love to me in ways I've asked for. What changed it? I don't know. I really don't. Now that he has made some changes, I can see clearly that I've got sexually related problems too. Sometimes I distract myself and think negative thoughts while making love. It's hard for me to let go, to surrender fully."

Carla's seven years with Joe have taught her a lot. Her beliefs are changing. She used to think that if sex wasn't just right she would never stay in a relationship, because sex is so important to her. But Carla stayed on in spite of a powerful urge to run. As a result, she learned that bad times do end, grief ends, anger ends. She now knows that Joe can change, she can change, and that she can be patient and live with a less than perfect sex life. On top of all that, she and Joe firmly believe that they can survive whatever life brings them. They already have survived.

As the years go by the older woman/younger man couple is sexually like any other. For some, sexual interest wanes. A few younger men turn away from their aging wives toward younger women. Some aging women try desperately to keep looking youthful in order to remain sexually attractive. Some older women accept marriages in which their younger husbands have other sexual partners. This was not the case of our interviewees, but we did hear about such couples from them and from other sources.

On the other hand, some couples maintain a lively sex life. Several couples who had been married for more than ten years reported a continuing delightful sex relationship even though the first intensity was over. Several couples told us they had gone through the process of working out agreements about how often to have sex. Mike and Mary Bayer, for instance, have a new baby, and his birth has altered their sex life. As mothers of infants usually do, Mary became focused on the baby's needs, and Mike got less of her attention. As she is easily distracted by the baby's cry in the night, Mike and Mary now face the challenge of working out when and how to develop the time and privacy to continue their sex life.

The durability of any relationship is based, not on age compatibility, but on the willingness of each person to commit him- or herself to solving problems. Sex problems, like money, power, and communication problems, are solvable if each person is willing to be flexible. The greater the maturity of each member of the couple, the greater the odds for working out agreements.

The older woman/younger man couple will face all the normal problems in their sex lives that any other couple does. Their success in solving these problems will depend on the strength of the other areas of their relationship, their friendship, their ability to solve disagreements, their tolerance of distress, and their commitment to one another.

Nearly all of the couples we interviewed report satisfying sex lives. They are well past the honeymoon period. We believe the successful reports are due to a feeling of genuine camaraderie and a generally relaxed, playful attitude toward sex. Older women/younger men couples have a lot of fun together. Good sex thrives on relaxation and spontaneity.

10 ·

THE QUESTION OF CHILDREN

When a younger man commits himself to a life with an older woman, there are important decisions to be made about having children. The older woman often comes complete with offspring; if the younger man wants her, he has to be prepared to take the whole package. A number of the men we interviewed had young children of their own. As a result, the older woman is sometimes faced with the possibility of raising a second family. However, the major problem that must be dealt with early in the relationship is whether or not this couple is going to have a child of their own.

We think that this is an issue on which both partners must reach an agreement before deciding on a committed relationship. If the younger man has a strong desire for children of his own and the older woman does not want to have another child, they are dealing with a nonnegotiable issue. If the question of having children is not resolved early in the relationship, it will become a major bone of contention, causing guilt and frustration in both partners. We cannot stress this point enough. The decision whether to have a child or not has serious implications for any marriage where one partner does not already have a child of his or her own, regardless of the age difference. Older woman/younger man couples are no more exempt than any other couple from intense feelings about this issue. Both need to be quite clear about where they stand on the subject. The couples we've interviewed have had a variety of responses to this problem.

For instance, Anna and Steven have lived together for about six months. Anna is forty and Steven is thirty. Steven was previously married to a woman with four children, but he has none of his own. However, he thinks of his former wife's children as his own. Anna has never married, has no children, and a few years ago she had a complete hysterectomy. Children mean a lot to Steven, and having them with Anna is obviously out. During our last interview with them, Steven told us that his ex-wife had moved away and, in addition, had denied him access to her children. He was still stunned when he told us about it. Anna felt that his distress might have considerable effect on their relationship. Steven reluctantly agreed. Recently, we heard that the relationship had broken up.

Most of the people whom we have interviewed have settled the question of a child of their own prior to marriage. When Doug Randall, twenty-six, met Peggy Barstow, thirty-nine, their decision to marry had to include some very serious thinking about the question of children. Peggy already had six children from a previous marriage. That was ten years ago. The Randalls have now been married for seven years, and only two of Peggy's children are still at home. Three are away at school and one lives with his father and spends summers with the Randalls. At this time their respective ages range from twenty-two to fifteen years old.

Doug told us that he would have liked to have children of his own, but both he and Peggy decided against it, primarily because of Peggy's age. In addition, at the time they were married, Peggy's children were still quite young and Doug had about as much as he could handle getting used to being a full-time parent to Peggy's brood. "Actually," Peggy informed us, "what he said to me at the time was, 'I hate to waste these marvelous genes of mine, but I think six is enough.' " Peggy feels that an infant at that point in their lives would have been a very heavy burden on their relationship and on the other children. Yet she thinks that only a very mature person could accept a relationship alone as meaning more to him than passing his name down to posterity. In Peggy's mind, that very mature person is obviously Doug.

We agree with Peggy. This is probably one of the most significant decisions a man must make in his lifetime. Some of the men we have interviewed, like Doug, would have loved to have children of their own. However, in many instances, younger men chose to go ahead with the relationship even if there was to be no child of their own blood. Many of these marriages, as we have already mentioned, come complete with the women's children from a previous marriage. Even though the younger men often have become very involved with these children, only time will tell whether they will have serious regrets about not having children of their own.

Peter Levin, thirty-one, who lives with forty-six-year-old Susan Howard and her children, feels that he has dealt satisfactorily with the issue of not having a child of his own. "It's a reality," says Peter, "and it's okay with me." Peter explains that he is very close to Susan's children, and the result is that at the tender age of thirty-one, he has become an expert on adolescent behavior. In addition, he has recently been presented with a niece and two nephews. "Now the terrific thing is that I can take care of them for as long as I'm enjoying them, and then return them to their parents when I've had enough." Peter grins. "It's an ideal way to experience babies.

Seriously, though, I think that feelings about having children of my own will come up again in my life. When that time comes, I'll have to deal with them. But as far as I can see, having a child of my own is not a major concern for me."

A few of the men we have interviewed have told us, in no uncertain terms, that they never saw children as part of their own life plans. They are willing to accept into their own lives the children of the women they love, but they have no desire for children of their own. Claire, thirty-eight, who has children from a previous marriage, and Sean, thirty, explain the choices they made about having children together when they began their relationship seven years ago.

Claire told Sean early in their relationship that since she already had three children, she was not about to have another. She wanted Sean to think it over carefully and decide how badly he wanted children of his own. She didn't want Sean to decide suddenly five years later that it was time for him to have a child and for their relationship to split on that issue. Sean had his answer ready even before Claire asked the question. "I don't ever want a child," he informed Claire. "I've never thought of children as being important in my life." Claire was not completely convinced. "He's young," she thought to herself; "he doesn't know what he's talking about."

But life has its own way of playing tricks on people. About three years ago one of Claire's children died in an accident. A natural part of parental grief is the desire to replace the lost child with a new baby. Claire thought seriously of having another child at that point, but Sean was adamantly opposed. He said to Claire, "If there's a new child, I don't even want to be in this relationship. Your two oldest children are almost grown. My dream is just to be alone with you after they've moved out."

Claire and Sean came close to separating over that issue. "It's so strange," Claire mused, "I thought the problem would be that he would eventually want a child, and then it turned out to be me. But we're not going to have a child together."

The majority of couples we interviewed have decided not to have children together. They explain their decisions in various ways. For instance, certain couples pointed out that there have always been childless marriages, some due to infertility and some to choice. They also felt that in the move toward zero population growth, the childless family unit will not be unusual. Many women who already have children feel finished with that part of their lives. They don't care to repeat the childbearing and -raising process. Their husbands, or the men they live with, seem satisfied with their stepchildren. A few of the men have expressed the same thoughts Sean Enderly did. They are not particularly interested in the care and raising of children. They would rather put the same energy into their marriages. Sometimes, both partners have career commitments or a life-style that precludes children. They prefer to focus their attention on each other.

Women who don't already have children generally feel more pressure than their men do to produce one. They tend to experience more guilt and to struggle more intensely with the question of having a child. Despite the popularity of the zero population growth concept, society still expects couples to procreate. Women, in particular, still find it difficult to resist the pressures of their conditioning.

Kelly Watson is a thirty-nine-year-old film producer. She has fought long and hard to get to this point in her career. One of the many rewards of her struggle is the executive-size salary that goes with her job. Kelly is married to Seth Shaler, an attorney who, at thirty-one, is just starting up the career ladder. Right now, their combined salaries allow them to live very comfortably. Kelly feels that she's earned this luxury and isn't especially anxious to give it up. For Kelly, having a child at this time in her life might mean really cutting back financially and giving up a lot of things she has worked for, including her professional status.

Kelly told us, "I don't think I ever really wanted children, not in the way most of the people I knew wanted children. Occasionally, I thought it would be nice to have a child but I never had a driving passion about it. Seth and I have thought about it. We've talked about it a lot. We will have to decide fairly soon, within the next year or two, or we probably won't have children at all."

Kelly and Seth have a difficult decision to make. It is highly probable that children will not fit into their life scheme.

Barbara Fein is a successful writer. Jeff Courtney, her husband, is a free-lance photographer and documentary filmmaker. Their individual careers involve a lot of travel time, and sometimes just having to pick up and go without much warning. Often they are separated for weeks or months at a time. Barbara shared with us her indecision about whether or not to have a child.

"This is the only area I've ever discovered where the older woman/younger man thing really bothers me. I'm thirty-eight now; I've never had a child. I probably never will, but I'm still not sure whether I want to have one. Sometimes I think they just don't fit into my life. Forget it; it would be selfish . . . and foolish. At other times I think, 'Oh, but I'd be a good mother; I could bring up a wonderful child.' Jeff has never wanted children. But he could change his mind. He could hit thirty-five, be well established, and suddenly say to himself, 'Yes, I'd like to have a family; I feel ready for it now.' Thirty-five is a perfectly ripe age to decide that. But when he's thirty-five, I'll be forty-three. I'm afraid that if he ever decides he wants a kid, I'll be too old to carry it."

Jeff interrupted. "I've never had any desire to have children. It would be difficult for our life-style."

Barbara added, "Even our cats are difficult. Our younger

kitten went and got pregnant on us. She's going to have the babies right when I am ready to leave. But at least you can leave a pet with a friend or at the vet's. You can't do that with a child. It's really hard to leave our cats here for four months; we couldn't ever leave a child for that long."

Deliberately choosing a way of life that doesn't include children is more difficult for some people than for others. If neither of the partners has ever had strong feelings of wanting children, life can go on without either the man or the woman feeling any great sense of deprivation. People tend not to miss very much what they have never experienced.

For a woman who already has experienced motherhood, the decision may be more difficult. If she is still well within the limits of her childbearing years, her decision not to have another child with her younger husband may feel very arbitrary to him. Liz Stefano's daughter was eleven when Liz married Paul. Liz was thirty-five, still young enough to bear another child comfortably. Paul was twenty-five and believed he did not want to raise children. Liz had absolutely no intentions of raising another child.

"One is plenty," she told us. Paul knew that marriage to Liz would mean giving up the idea of a child of his own. "This is not the kind of problem where people can work out a compromise," said Liz. "Either you have a baby or you don't." The Stefanos agreed to a no-baby contract before they were married, but they told us that after four years of marriage, they still have moments of private doubt about their decision.

The couples interviewed have expressed different points of view about the question of having children of their own. Very few older woman/younger man couples have a traditional attitude about children as a part of family and marriage. Almost everyone we talked to felt that the lack of a child of their own did not present an unresolvable obstacle to a healthy relationship. Yet several of the women we interviewed told us of feeling some guilt about not wanting to have any more children. They were concerned about their husbands' not having children of their own. But only two of the couples we spoke to planned on having a child together.

One of those couples is Shoshana and Robbie Wise. Shoshana, who arrived from Israel two years ago, is thirty-five and Robbie is twenty-three. Shoshana has a twelve-year-old son, who recently came to live with them in the United States. She is quite confident that she can handle both a career and another child. The Wises are in complete agreement that a child of their own is extremely important to them and Shoshana has always assumed that she would have a second child.

The idea that she would want to have a fourth child was initially surprising to Mary Bayer. She was thirty-nine when she married twenty-four-year-old Mike. At that time, her youngest child was fifteen years old and her oldest was twenty. We asked the Bayers why they had decided to have a child together. To Mike, having a child with Mary symbolized the completeness of their relationship. "I wanted a child very much, but I didn't expect her to have one." He was a little taken aback when Mary announced that she would really like to have a baby with him.

Mary had experienced easy pregnancies with her first three children, but she admits that she was a little frightened of this pregnancy because she was older. "My pregnancy was a little rougher this time," she confessed. However, she felt that it was so important for her and Mike to have a baby together that she could live with the discomfort. And after three boys, Mary was convinced that she would give birth to another beautiful boy. She was right.

Two months after our initial interview, Adam Bayer was born. The wonderful romantic fantasy of having a baby with someone you love became, as always, a mixed blessing. We talked to Mary Bayer when Adam was about six months old and asked for her thoughts on being the mother of an infant at forty.

Mary's remarks reflect what most mothers of a new baby would experience plus the additional stress that being older causes. To begin with, Adam was born by Cesarian section, which Mary had half-suspected would happen, even though her doctor had originally felt she would have a normal delivery. "I found recovery from the pregnancy took a lot longer than I expected," Mary said. She didn't lose weight as fast as she had after the other births and would periodically become depressed about it.

Mary gave us a wry smile. "I had made up my mind when Adam was about six weeks old that I was going to go bike riding. But I couldn't get into anything to wear on the bike. Finally, I put on Mike's shorts and one of his really big sweatshirts. I was bummed out because I had tried on everything of mine. I came down the stairs and Mike said, 'Oh honey, you look so cute,' and I snapped, 'Don't be ridiculous!' I went out the door and I started pedaling my bike and I was crying, because at that moment I felt really ugly."

We asked Mary if the baby had affected her relationship with Mike. "Definitely," she said. "I know Mike sometimes feels neglected." Mike admitted to her that he finds himself a little torn between resenting the time that Adam takes and then feeling guilty about resenting it. Mary told us that it never occurred to her in her first marriage that her husband may have felt left out because of the attention she gave the children. It also never occurred to her to ask for his help. "Mike has always given Adam his bottle at night," she said, "and now he bathes the baby and entertains him while I make dinner."

Mary has been much more observant of Adam's development and Mike shares this excitement with her. She doesn't remember noticing those things when she was younger. Mary's college education included courses in child psychology and child development. She is looking forward to watching Adam go through each change.

Mary, at forty-one, has the advantage of being more aware of potential problems in her life. Because she has gone through childrearing before and learned some new things about children's development, she is likely to head off difficulties by facing them sooner. She knows what to expect from babies and can be more patient with Adam. Her maturity has given her more understanding of Mike's feelings. But most of all, Mary's experience of motherhood with Mike at her side is a considerable improvement over her first time around. Mike commented, "Mary was in a loveless marriage for a long time. I want her to relive her life with a man who loves her."

Some of the people we've interviewed have told us that they are thinking of trying something a little innovative in family styles. In some instances, both partners are willing to share equal responsibility in child care or to employ a baby nurse. An older woman who is a successful moneymaker can afford to pay for full-time, professional care for a child by herself. A much talked-about alternative is the house-husband. The mother can bear a child and the father can assume full responsibility for the care and raising of the child while the mother continues in her work. There probably aren't many men who have the stamina to withstand the kind of social pressure that would result from their rejection of the accepted male role.

Thirty-year-old Nachmy Bronstein is one of those men. His ten-year-older wife, Phyllis Chesler, gave birth to their son, Ariel, in 1978. While Ms. Chesler continues in her career as feminist author and psychologist, Bronstein takes care of their child. In an article from the magazine *US*, Ms. Chesler told an interviewer, "He does it better than me. Our strengths are different."[1]

A colleague of ours told us about her woman client, aged thirty-four, who married an attorney ten years younger than she. The client was a widow who had two children, ten and twelve years old. The young husband told her that he didn't want any children of his own. The woman was at the time studying law herself, and they agreed on a no-children contract. Six years later, when the wife's children were older and she was really moving ahead in her own career, the husband discovered that he really did want a child of his own, after all. The wife was willing to have a child but did not want to be responsible for its care. They decided that the husband would either take care of the child himself or provide mutually satisfactory child care.

For about a year, the husband took care of the baby himself. The child is now three years old and for the last two years the family has employed a full-time housekeeper to care for him. The father says that he enjoyed part of the experience very much. One of the results is that the little boy demands far more of his father than of his mother. But apparently the father has decided that he does not want to have the major share of parental responsibility a second time.

Since so many of the women in older woman/younger man relationships have children of their own, the younger man quickly faces the question that most same-age divorced persons face: namely, what to do about the new partner's children. For many older woman/younger man couples, there is no childless honeymoon period. The younger man has to start making adjustments to family life almost immediately. If he had any fantasies about being the one and only, the realities of coping with his lover's ready-made family will dispel them right away. Most younger men contemplating marriage to an older woman realize that they will have to make room in their lives for her children. Several older women with grown children have told us that they also had to adapt to their new husband's offspring, additional household members they would have preferred to do without.

One of the first problems that can confront the younger man is seductive overtures from the woman's female children. The situation is confusing. Sometimes, when stepfather and stepdaughter are closer in age than stepfather and mother, it can be a sticky issue. Susan Howard, forty-six, talked about the first time her daughter met Peter Levin. Betsy was sixteen and Peter was twenty-six. Susan had asked Betsy to answer the door because she was on the phone. Betsy came into her room a few minutes later and asked, "Who's the fox?" Susan said Peter was a very nice man she had met and wanted to know if Betsy liked him. Betsy replied, "If you don't want him, throw him my way."

Susan told us that at the time Betsy was at an age where her gonads were exploding wildly in all directions and she was sending out sexual signals to anything male in sight. However, as Peter became a fixture in Susan's home, Betsy's flirtatiousness calmed down. Peter laughed. "I developed a very brotherly attitude toward her. It eventually turned her off."

There is always a possibility that teenage children will behave seductively toward any new grownup in their lives. Seductiveness is usually a testing of the new person who is going to live in an intimate relationship with the family. Boys tend to be as seductive to a young stepmother as girls are to a young stepfather. Even a stepparent of the parent's own age will generate flirtatious activity. Seductive behavior toward a stepparent is a part of the normal settling-in process.

Although the child's sexual confusion may be heightened when the stepparent is considerably younger than the original parent, the problem is dealt with in exactly the same way that it would be handled by a couple equal in age. The younger stepparent takes full responsibility for making sure that he or she does not send out sexual signals that further confuse the issue, and gently but firmly refuses to encourage the youngster's seductive behavior.

We asked a thirty-eight-year-old woman if she was uncomfortable about her twenty-two-year-old lover's being around her eighteen-year-old daughter. "No," she said, "and I'm extremely sensitive to that. I have dated men my own age who have been attracted to my younger daughter, and I can't accept that. I don't feel that at all with my younger man. He's not remotely interested."

Jenna Trenton's younger son, Andrew, was living with her when her relationship with Barry, twenty-six years younger, began. When their friendship turned into a love affair, Jenna told Andrew about the change in the relationship. He was pleased with the idea, as he was fond of Barry, and he worked it out from there.

But Jenna also told us of a forty-three-year-old woman friend who has been having an affair with a younger man for over six years. Her children, who are seventeen and nineteen, did not know about the sexual aspect of the relationship. Her friends, who did know, had been sworn to secrecy on the subject. Recently, someone new to the group mentioned the affair in the presence of the older daughter. The girl ran out of the room screaming hysterically, "No, she isn't; no, she isn't."

Not informing at least the older children in the family about the sexual status of a relationship can often result in painful confusion and distrust of the parent as well as the lover. Possibly the daughter in the previous story has been having romantic fantasies about her mother's lover. Or perhaps sexual matters are not mentioned in her home. Whatever the explanation may be, it is generally a good idea in an older woman/younger man relationship to make sexual boundaries very clear to the woman's children. This is as helpful to boys as it is to girls. Most younger men who live with older women have reported that early in the relationship their women's sons may go through a period of being suffocatingly protective of Mommy.

There are other problems that come up in a child's adaptation to a stepparent. One's offspring may be used to having the exclusive attention of a single parent and really resent sharing their parent with a new person.

A forty-eight-year-old woman described her daughter's adaptation to her lover, twenty-three, after they had decided to live together. "When we first started our relationship, my boyfriend and my daughter, who are a month apart in age, were buddy-buddy, and then all of a sudden it was little daggers at each other. Finally, my daughter said to me, 'You know, Mom, it's like you brought a new baby home from the hospital.' Now, she had not been living with me; I had been alone for many years. All of a sudden I didn't have a lot of time to go running around with her, and she missed it. It wasn't too long after that that the two of them started getting it back together, because I made it clear to them that that was really important to me. They were the two dearest people in my life, and I wanted them to get along."

Getting one's children used to the fact that a parent may not be able to give the same amount of time and attention as she previously gave takes patience and understanding. It takes a while to work out the living relationships in a newly blended family.

Simone Hartley, forty-four, said she felt there were times when her twenty-year-old lover was very jealous of her nineteen-year-old-daughter. She mentioned that Robert had come from a family with very little money and equally little opportunity for education or advancement. Simone thought that Robert was probably comparing his own life to that of her daughter. "Here was my daughter learning to drive, traveling to France and through the United States, and going to college," Simone said. "I think Robert was jealous of my daughter's opportunities, and I can understand his feelings."

Parents who have fought their way up from relative poverty can be resentful of their children's offhand acceptance of the things the parents struggled to obtain. They are still wishing that someone had given them what they are able to provide for their children. It would not be surprising for a young step-parent to be resentful about seeing someone his own age get opportunities he never had.

Not only can the younger man be jealous of what is freely given to the woman's children, but through his alliance with an older woman, he has often been catapulted into the re-sponsibilities of parenthood a little ahead of his time. As a result, he can be unduly hard on the irresponsible behavior or adolescent defensiveness of the children he lives with.

Peter Levin was twenty-six when he first had to come to terms with his relationship with Sam, Susan Howard's thirteen-year-old son. Peter recalls that he felt as if he were picking on Sam all the time. "After a while," Peter said, "I realized that since this was my first time as a parent, I was simply doing the same thing all parents classically do with their kids. I was supersensitive to seeing Sam do the things I didn't like about myself. I was also jealous that I was not allowed to get away with those things myself anymore."

Outsiders often question the younger man's ability to deal with teenage boys in the home who may not be much younger than he. Will the boy resent the younger man if he tries to impose his authority in the household? Will they accept him as a substitute father figure? A major part of Mary Bayer's decision to have a child with Mike was based on Mike's will-ingness to take her three sons in hand. "Since my sons have gotten older, they have been really hard for me to raise, especially in the last four years when I've been by myself," Mary says.

Although other people may wonder if Mike has the capability to cope with Mary's boys, Mike himself has few qualms about the situation. He obviously likes the boys very much and is concerned about them. He is patient with the vagaries of adolescence, helps them with their homework, and sees to it that they don't talk back to Mary.

He talked about how he sees his role with the boys. "They are children and I am an adult," Mike said. "I understand that they don't want to be dominated or told what to do, but they live under my roof and I pay the bills. I'm not going to let them boss me around." After some testing, Mary's oldest son, who is two years younger than Mike, moved out. Mike approves. "He's old enough to be his own man, have a good job, and find a lady of his own." Mike feels that he can be a positive influence in the boys' lives and takes his responsibilities as a stepparent seriously.

When people ask questions about children in the older woman/younger man relationship, they usually assume that if there is any difficulty, it will be between the young stepfather and the children. The women, of course, being naturally maternal, will simply take any adjustment to their men's off-spring in stride. Not necessarily true. Approximately one-third of the men we interviewed had a child or children from a previous marriage. We talked to some of the women who were trying to adapt their lives to include the children of the younger man. Attitudes surfaced that were different from those of the men.

Although adapting to the woman's children often presented unexpected difficulties, most of the men we interviewed were enthusiastic about becoming part of a family and were obviously fond of the children. Younger men who are not interested in accepting the woman's children usually don't commit themselves to living with her, let alone consider marriage. But the attitudes of several of the women toward their younger men's children were different. Most of these women had spent a large part of their adult life raising their own children and weren't keen on the idea of repeating the experience. However, circumstances occasionally occurred in which the father had custody of his child. If the woman wanted to live with the father, she took the child as well.

In one of these situations, the older woman/younger man couple worked out an interesting solution. Marilyn Sterling is forty-three, divorced, and has an eighteen-year-old son. About two years ago she met Bill Dunnigan, thirty-four, also divorced. Bill has one child, a little boy five years old. Marilyn and Bill dated, fell in love, and after working at a number of the problems that confront older woman/younger man relationships, decided to live together.

This year Marilyn's son left for college and she settled into enjoying the free space that occurs when one's children finally leave home. No one but another person who has had the full responsibility for the welfare of a child for many years can know what that first luscious flash of freedom feels like. No timetable to keep, meals to make, endless nagging about homework, bedmaking, dirty dishes in the sink, and curfews. For women who have been trying to balance a job and child care for a large part of their lives, just the possibility of sitting in a chair, staring into space, knowing that you don't have to clear the TV snack dishes out of the sink for the third time in one evening is a marvelous feeling.

At that point in Marilyn's life, Bill's wife called up and said that she had decided to move back to her home city, clear across the country. She offered Bill full custody of their little boy, and Bill really wanted his child to live with him. "Don't get me wrong," Marilyn told us; "I like the child. He's a nice little person, healthy and well behaved. But the first thing that hit me was, 'No, not again. I just got finished with that. I don't want to go through all that again.' " Marilyn thought seriously at that time of ending her living relationship with Bill. She was extremely reluctant to give up her new-found privacy, but, more important, there was no way she was going to accept the major responsibility for raising another child.

"It's not that I feel I'm too old," Marilyn explained. "Hell, I've got enough energy for five children. I've been a grade-school teacher for ten years and I love my work and the kids. It's just that I don't choose to have the experience of full-time motherhood again."

After much exploration of alternative possibilities, Bill and Marilyn came up with a plan. Bill would be the one to shift gears, changing his job so that he could take the primary re-sponsibility for his child. He would arrange and be available for all doctors' appointments, baby-sitters, car pooling, and after-school activities. If his son was ill, it would be his re-sponsibility either to take time off from work or find adequate care for him. Vacations would be handled the same way. Marilyn, in turn, would provide whatever help she was willing to give. So far the arrangement has been effective, and as a result of Bill's willingness to work at being a full-time father, Marilyn finds herself willing to do more than she had originally planned.

"I actually feel more like a grandmother than a stepmother. Not because of my age, but because of the situation. Because I am not totally stuck with the endless tasks and discipline of child care, I have a lot of energy for the fun things with him. Going to the park, playing card games, making cookies. I think I feel like many grandparents, having a cute little boy to show off without having to do all the scutwork."

The blended family system is not always easy to work out. Most women are already familiar with children, know what they are like and what to realistically expect from them. If a man brings his own children into their living situation, the woman has at least some idea of what to do and can generally cope with adapting to additional children.

But for fifty-year-old Amy Carson, children are an absolute mystery. She has lived with Mark, thirty-eight, for three years. Mark is divorced and has two little girls who usually come and stay every other weekend. The problem with Mark's children is a switch on the majority of older women/younger men family situations.

Amy explained what she was feeling. "There is some reason why in fifty years I chose never to have children, although I've always gotten along with children well, as long as they're quiet. If they're not going to be quiet, then they should just go away. I find the sound unbearable. When Mark's children are around this much, it gets noisy.

"There's a point where I don't know what to do with them. I don't know how to relate to them, and it takes up too much of my time and space. They're Mark's children, and I want him to have them here, but I feel that I have an obligation to make them a second home, which I don't really want to do. My image of myself as second mother is a lady with an apron making them cookies, and that is not me at all."

Mark's older daughter is nine years old and the younger one is seven. We asked Amy and Mark how they organized the time that they spend with the children. Mark told us, "Sometimes I'll do things with them and sometimes I'll take them out. Last time they were here, we were together; the time before, I took them out for the whole day and then we came home for supper."

Amy added, "Being together means that Mark's in the front building things with them and I'm in bed with a book. When they come to me I will talk with them very pleasantly and when I get tired of talking with them I tell them I'm

going back to my book." Mark explained that they had tried
to work out a system of having the children one at a time, but
Mark and Amy go through spurts of traveling that are part of
their jobs. When that happens and Mark's been away for a
while, it doesn't seem fair to the girls not to take them both.
So the system breaks down.

We sat in a small silence and then Amy started to laugh
to herself. "You know," she said, "my ex-husband thinks this
is hysterical. He turned up one day and said to me, 'Do you
realize we avoided having children all these years and now the
lady I'm living with has three children and Mark has two?'
My ex-husband handles it differently, though. He lives in the
front of the apartment and the kids live in the back." Mark
chimed in at this point, "Sometimes, he may come out to
eat." We laughed and then Amy sighed, "The trouble is that
when two very normal small children come around wanting
attention, I really don't know what to do."

Although we empathized with Mark and Amy's concern
about his children's place in their lives, we were also amused
by the situation. It's such a complete reversal of the normal
sex roles. In particular, Mark and Amy's relationship with his
children tends to shake up two major cultural beliefs: first,
that young men who are attracted to women older than they
are looking for mothers, and second, that all women are automatically, intuitively maternal. Amy could not be less interested in motherhood. Mark is the capable parent, taking
complete responsibility for the care of his children when they
come to stay with him. Amy sees as much of the children as
she feels she can tolerate.

We see the way Amy and Mark deal with the children as a
perfectly acceptable method of handling the blended family.
Amy has a distinct life-style of her own that has never included
children. However, it is all right with Amy for the children
to be in her and Mark's home as long as her need for privacy

is respected and the children understand that she needs a certain amount of time to be alone.

When twenty-eight-year-old Doug Randall married, he acquired a forty-one-year-old wife and six children. To what extent had his age been a source of problems with Peggy's kids? "I'm not so sure that age was a factor at all," Doug said. Both he and Peggy think that whatever problems arose about him and the children had to do with stepparenting and the formation of a new family. Doug took a long period of time before committing himself to marrying Peggy and her family. He needed to have his feelings about the children clear before assuming responsibility for them. And when the family is large, it helps to have a stepfather who is willing to share some of the responsibilities of child care.

The people in older woman/younger man relationships have chosen a variety of ways to handle the question of children as a part of their relationship. But one characteristic in these relationships has come up over and over again. In the majority of the families we've interviewed, the couple cooperates extensively in sharing the care of the children. Most of these younger men have taken far more day-to-day responsibility for the children with whom they live than the male parent usually does in the traditional family. And while the men are giving more of themselves to the personal care of home, wife, and children, many of the women are taking a larger responsibility as breadwinners for the family.

11 ·

THE SHARED EXPERIENCE

ONCE A YOUNGER MAN AND AN OLDER WOMAN AT-
tract one another, what is it that keeps them together? What
do they give? What do they get? Is what they give connected
to their age difference? What are the problems that will arise
from a disparity in experience level? As we interviewed we
looked for patterns. At least two-thirds of our interviewees
have a unique, yet predictable, pattern of relating that is a
factor of the man's youth and the woman's greater age.

Young men contribute what they have in abundance, the
energy that is usually associated with youth. A forty-eight-
year-old woman who lives with a twenty-three-year-old man
says, "I associate energy with younger men, mental as well as
physical energy, because I have a tremendously energetic kind
of personality. Men my age or older seem to drag me down
with their crotchetiness. Just when I'm ready to get up and go
they want to fall asleep in front of the TV set."

This older woman needs a man who can match her highly
active pace. She is like many of the women we spoke to who
have lives filled with ambitious work goals, varied projects,

and adventurous dreams. Many young men laughed when we asked if they were afraid their older women partners would not keep up with them later in life. They said they were more afraid of not keeping up with the women.

Another quality that women admire about their younger men partners is their relatively uncontaminated idealism. Several women commented that they deeply appreciated their mates' personal integrity. Most of the women we've interviewed often experience men their own age as world-weary, disillusioned, and cynical. One woman administrator told us angrily that she was tired of being told that her ethical system was a sign of immaturity. Her supervisor had told her to falsify certain reports to the government. When she resisted doing so, he said, "Come on, baby, grow up. Everyone knows that's how it's done in this world." "It's one thing to accept as a reality that a lot of people are crooked," she said to us; "it's another thing to insist that dishonesty is maturity."

A younger man, still idealistic, still socially conscious, is immensely appealing to the older woman who is going through her own radicalization, who is fighting to maintain her own personal integrity in the world. In addition, young men often are passionate enthusiasts. Liz, thirty-eight, says of Paul Stefano, twenty-eight, "Love of life. Isn't that the title of a soap opera? Well, that's Paul too. He's so pleased by the smallest things: a ride, flowers, colors in the sky, a special food, or a song. He practically jumps up and down at the prospect of some adventure. Things are rarely boring. 'You want to ride to New Mexico on the motorcycle?' he says to me. 'You want to go out for coffee (at three A.M.)?' "

Nearly every woman we interviewed said life was more fun with a younger man. As we packed up our tape recorder one evening, forty-five-year-old Marta said, "I must tell you this before you leave. I've never had so much fun with a man before. We clean house together; we go to the market to-gether. Living together is like play."

The most striking feature older women/younger men couples have in common is their ability to have fun together. Younger men bring out the more playful aspects of the older woman's personality, saying, "Let go, have fun, it's okay."

Paul and Liz Stefano say they laugh a lot together. One of them starts a joke and the other keeps it going. Liz says, "I want to share my life with someone who loves to play. Paul has held onto the childlike part of his nature, the ability to play, to feel, to intuit, and to risk. He brings out the child part of me. I have already got a strong analytic, rational side. The four years we have been together have been the most dar-ing, creative, and productive years of my life. When I try to think why this is so, I keep thinking balance — balance. The fun we have is somehow freeing. It is the balance to the secur-ity of our marriage and the seriousness of my work. The repeti-tive chores of family life are lightened with play. Sometimes we do this just by sharing the work. Sometimes we do it by getting silly immediately following a dreadful job. Playing gets us through hard times; it makes the tedious times better and the good times terrific."

Liz says it well. She and Paul have found a way to lift the level of their experience in life. As family therapists we find that many couples divorce when all the fun has gone out of their lives together. When there is very little pleasure and a lot of strife, each feels it is not worth the effort. Play is vital to a healthy personality and to a healthy relationship. Play and work are not necessarily mutually exclusive. From the playing of the mind come creativity, art, and invention. Un-fortunately, in our culture, fun is often defined as frivolity. And what is frivolous is seen as useless or trivial. Actually, frivolity is life-sustaining. Older women/younger men couples, with their positive attitude toward play, are a good model for all other couples.

A young man contributes youthful energy, idealism, and enthusiastic play. An older woman has experience in life. Women of thirty-five and older are apt to be balancing a career and the care of children, often without a husband. They have self-knowledge, goals, and a certain centeredness that is unavailable to younger women. If they are divorced, they have faced a struggle to become independent, perhaps for the first time in their lives, at the age of thirty-five or forty or fifty. They have worked hard to become the persons they are. Some are looking for partners, some are resigned to being alone, and some are still recovering from the breakup of a long first marriage. Often the woman has been a lifelong responsible caretaker. She brings stability to the relationship.

The older woman and the younger man often meet at a time when each is ready to expand his or her style to include the style of the other. The woman is ready to learn to have fun, to let go of her hyperresponsibility, and to allow more pleasure into her life. After a childhood of rebellious behavior and/or a searching, rootless period in his twenties, the young man is ready to sink anchor, to enjoy the pleasures of family life, and to take on more responsibility.

Mike Bayer, twenty-six, told us about his wild, rebellious teens, his years of fighting, getting into trouble, and struggling with his parents. We heard this story a number of times from the younger men we interviewed, but in Mike's case we had the additional testimony of his mother, Anita. Anita described the powerfully positive impact of Mike's marriage to Mary. Mike had been nervous, without direction. When he met Mary he calmed down, settled by Mary's admiration and her quiet sense of order. He eagerly took on the immense job of helping her with her teenage sons. Here he describes how helping her helped him.

"Mary's divorce had upset the boys. There was a lot of turmoil. The boys had trouble with their schoolwork, so I helped them at home. There was a lack of discipline and too much disrespect for Mary. I refused to allow that to go on. So I just lifted some of that burden off Mary and that gave me self-respect, let me assume a responsible role."

At least a third of the men we spoke to had a history like Mike's. There is something about older women that makes it possible for younger men to take a more responsible place in life with less pressure than they might feel with a woman their own age. Several men mentioned they had felt trapped by younger women who put pressure on them to make money and have children. One young man said he needed an anchor but not a ball and chain.

David, thirty-six, told us that Tina, forty-seven, contributes stability and self-confidence to the relationship. He maintains that the value of an older woman as a partner derives from the fact that she's been through a lot, has figured out what she wants to do, has a plan for herself, and doesn't have the ambivalence that a younger woman might have about her role in society. David says he himself is often confused and he doesn't want to be around confused people. His work takes him into dealings with difficult, creative people, all the more reason why he needs Tina's stability.

Older women and younger men relationships, at their best, are based on friendship, a mix of companionship, emotional support, appreciation, and devotion. What is friendship, essentially, but the coming together of kindred spirits to help and enjoy one another? Two hundred years ago a young Frenchman named Benjamin Constant de Rebecque fell in love with a woman who was forty-seven. In a letter to a friend, he described their meeting. "The cast of her mind delighted me and we spent whole days and nights in talk. She could be very cutting in her criticisms of the ideas and personalities that surrounded her. I, too, was given to mocking. So we were a perfect match. Madame de Charrières' view of life was so original and so very much her own; her intellect was so power-ful, and her superiority to the average human being so marked and certain that I, twenty years old, and as much of an oddity and an enemy of sham as herself, found in her company a sheer joy such as I had never known before."[1]

Constant captures the sense of intimacy, the feeling of being kindred spirits, that is characteristic of the very happy older woman/younger man relationships, and although like-minded companionship is invaluable in life, like-minded does not necessarily mean identical. There is as much individual difference and disagreement among older women/younger men couples as any other couples. Like-minded in this case means agreement on certain concepts such as a perception of the world, a life-style, and the value of each person to the other.

Tina talks about David's appreciation for her as she is. "I wouldn't like him if he were older than I am. One of the things I like about him is the way he thinks, and the way he thinks is the product of his generation. I was previously mar-ried to a man who was eighteen years older than I am and completely in the male ethic. It is a relief and refreshing to meet somebody who is free, not totally free by any means, but certainly not threatened when there is a discussion about who's going to do the dishes. My ex-husband and I used to have arguments all the time about the fact that I did all the housework, all my office work, and ran his life. I got tired of it and Matt just would not deal with this. So it was nice to meet someone who wasn't threatened by my being me and wanting less caretaking responsibility. David seems to think I am terrific the way I am. And I think one of David's attrac-tions for me is that he thinks I'm terrific. He's always re-establishing what I really am, because my ego suffers somewhat.

He reminds me of who I am and what I really want to do. I think that's been useful."

Instead of being in conflict, as she was with her former husband, Tina is in agreement with David on the need for sharing responsibilities. With David she feels free to get help, to get emotional support and attention to her needs.

When we asked a thirty-eight-year-old teacher what she thought her twenty-two-year-old husband liked about her, she replied, "If I have to guess, I would say it's probably because I'm more mature than a woman his age. I sense the space that he needs, probably more so than someone who is in her twenties, who is goal-oriented about marriage and children. We are compatible because I don't need that."

A twenty-two-year-old man described the ways in which he and his forty-seven-year-old wife are balanced. "She's at an age where she's been through the stage of definitely incorporating male traits which had been excluded. I'm at a stage where I'm strongly attempting to incorporate female traits; that's an inherent balance. She is at a place where she has professionally established herself and is very secure in her identity. She knows what she's good at. I'm in a stage where I am ambitiously expanding all over the place."

Mike Bayer describes his sense of being in tune with his wife. "Our minds are similar. Our ability to communicate, feel at ease, is similar. It's almost like our brainwaves are matching fingerprints. Her way of being is harmonious with mine. It takes in everything. I've found somebody who empathizes with me, understands and relates to things in the same way. The little things, her personality judgments, her evaluations of people, the way she makes her decisions. We connect well."

This series of quotes demonstrates a typical characteristic of successful relationships, the feeling of being in tune with one another. In two instances this harmonious feeling was directly connected to the age difference. That difference allows these individuals a greater freedom to be themselves. Many of the older women and the younger men we interviewed believe their age difference makes it easier for them to accept each other's unique behavior.

In a good marriage and in a good friendship, individuals cooperate. Each tries to provide the needed emotional or physical support. Many of the people we talked to had demanding, difficult careers. For such individuals emotional support is vital.

For example, Jeff and Barbara Courtney-Fein discussed a period of financial and emotional struggle. When Barbara, thirty-four, had an idea for a book that she was trying to write, Jeff, twenty-six, was putting together a book of his photography. There was very little money coming in. Barbara says that Jeff was enormously supportive during the writing of her book, even though he was very involved with his own work. Barbara calls herself a "middle-class worrier" about unpaid bills. About halfway through her book, she started to feel she should go out and get a job. She said to herself, "You don't sit home, write books, and be a bum when you could be out making money." Repeatedly, Jeff had to talk her out of her anxiety, convince her that writing a book was valid and worthwhile work that would be rewarded. "Something will come up," he'd say. "We'll eat; don't worry." It was tough, but they hung on to the end. Jeff believes that if Barbara had stopped to get a job, she wouldn't now be reaping both the emotional and financial rewards of being a published author.

Barbara's book has done very well. Still, she will not see the bulk of her money for quite a while. She has gone back to generating new ideas for books, screenplays, and stories. Again she has no regular job and again she feels guilty about taking the time off. Barbara says that every now and then Jeff has to lecture her about her guilt. "Look," he says, "you can't be creative if you don't take the time. It's not that you're being a bum. It's just hard to get into creative work. It takes time." Barbara is grateful that Jeff helps her keep on track with her goals. His positive attitude is just what she needs to balance her periodic pangs of guilt.

Since Jeff and Barbara had published at the same time, we wondered if there had been any difficulties between them. Did they feel jealous, competitive? Jeff is realistic about the fact that his book has a limited audience. He's very happy with the acceptance his book has had. Jeff told us, "The book was put together well and I have done well in promoting it. There's been no jealousy; I've never really felt conflict."

Barbara concurs. The subject of her book has a much wider audience than Jeff's. Therefore, it's being pushed more; there is more money behind it. There are times when she feels slightly self-conscious because of all the mail and clippings that come in because of her book. She's very sensitive to Jeff's feelings. She sweated over his book almost as much as he did. She doesn't want him to feel neglected because she's getting a lot more public attention than he is. Jeff, as usual, is reassuring. He is happy with the fact that both he and Barbara have brought out successful books. Recently, the Courtney-Feins have signed a lucrative contract to produce a book together.

Like Barbara and Jeff, many of the couples we interviewed spoke of giving one another emotional support, tolerance for the necessary sacrifices, and a surprising degree of devotion to each other's work goals.

Susan Howard, forty-six, and Peter Levin, thirty-one, are grateful for the opportunity to be with a partner who wants sex-role flexibility. Peter is freed from the need to take on the macho-boss role. Susan can give up the dependent-wife role. Each of them appreciates the ability of the other to play many roles. They use that developed skill to make their lives easier and more varied. They have encouraged one another's personal and professional growth. It hasn't all been easy. They have worked hard at learning how to bend and adjust to another's changing needs. Early in their relationship Susan was working full-time and simultaneously studying for a master's degree. Things were very tight. Peter stopped working and took over the care of their home, of Susan's children and of Susan herself, who was on a very demanding schedule. After two years on domestic duty Peter decided to return to school for his B.A. and M.A. degrees. By then Susan had finished her degree and had begun a book. During this period home chores were shared. Peter, of course, had less time to devote to Susan. Sometimes she missed the way it had been when he was taking care of everyone, but she was pleased to see Peter working toward his own goals. She was happy to see him gain the confidence that came with completing his graduate work and earning money.

Peter and Susan have struggled with the details of their lives together, adapted to each other's changing directions, and come out with many benefits. Each feels secure in the knowledge that the other can take over the responsibilities of any part of their lives. As life sends them opportunities or blows, they are certain that they can find a way to cope. They have given one another an opportunity to develop all the sides of themselves, an opportunity to learn new skills for living.

The fact that older women and younger men provide one another with the opportunity for role flexibility is not part of the mythology about older women/younger men couples. It was discussed frequently in the interviews but never in the questions of outsiders. But a question we heard often was "Doesn't the older woman act as a teacher to the younger man?" This is another belief that implies that the older woman is in a superior position to a younger man.

People who don't necessarily believe that the older woman/

younger man relationship is a mother-son affair often see the couple as teacher and student, instead. There seems to be a need to make one aspect the reason for the entire relationship.

For instance, a recurring theme in romantic literature is the platonic relationship with sexual overtones between a mature woman and a man young enough to be her son. The young man worships at the feet of the older woman, who is his mentor. He has secret sexual fantasies about her and she about him. At some point in the story their love is announced, consummated, and then renounced as inappropriate. The young man goes on his way, her image graven on his heart forever.

A professor of English in a southern California college told us, "Sometimes a very special relationship occurs between a teacher and a student. The student looks upon the teacher as his ideal; the teacher sees the student as her intellectual heir. To be adoringly emulated by a brilliant, sensitive young man is heady stuff. It is always tempting to slip from the role of the beloved mentor to the role of beloved mistress. Keeping the relationship platonic with these kinds of feelings going on can be terribly difficult."

Younger men have told us that an older woman's experience and professional expertise is often very helpful to them without necessarily being sexually connected. "But if a lady is smart and genuinely wants to help without talking down to me," said one young man, "then she'll probably turn me on regardless of her age." The men who have chosen older women as partners have additional points to make about the advantages of learning from an older woman.

A thirty-five-year-old factory owner who lives with a forty-five-year-old woman who runs a catering service says, "I can talk business with Janis. I can say, 'Hey, these are the problems at my office. What do you think I should do about it?' She'll tell me what she thinks I ought to do; she gives good advice.

She has the maturity behind what she's saying. I value her judgment. I've dated women who were twenty-three to women who are thirty-two. They don't have what it takes to make the kind of relationship I want and to give me the feedback I need. What I got from them was conversations about the secretary they went to lunch with, or that they settled two insurance claims today. Because Janis has her own business, she can give me feedback in those areas."

Another young man told us how his wife, who is twenty years older, helps him in his bureaucratic job. His wife has survived many years in the teaching profession. Patrick calls his wife from work, describes the latest intrigue, and then receives the benefit of her long experience. She is teaching him how to deal with the frustrations of office politics.

Older women do teach younger men about living fully. Jenna Trenton, fifty-four, has taught Barry Trenton, twenty-eight, how to live a rich, stimulating life, not by moralizing about it, but by her example. Jenna has nearly always done exactly what she wished. As a result her interests are many and varied. She has encouraged Barry to follow his own interests.

When Barry was asked if he had changed any in the three years he and Jenna had been together, he answered, "I think maybe I've gotten older. Not just three years older; maybe fifteen years older. For instance, I was thrust into a completely different society with no idea of its history. I had no idea what was happening in the United States in 1930 to 1939. I didn't know about Prohibition. I didn't know what the hell it was. Jenna lived through it. As a kid she smuggled bottles of hooch. So I've become a thirty-eight-year-old American rather than a twenty-eight-year-old Englishman. Before I lived with Jenna I used to come home from work and sit myself in front of the TV. We still watch TV but I also fly airplanes now; we were building one but we decided to sell it. I go out in the garage and fool around with electronics. I taught myself computer programming, which is very difficult without a computer."

People generally agree that an older woman probably has something to teach a younger man. But is it only one-sided? In spite of popular belief to the contrary, younger men instruct older women in many areas of life. An intelligent woman may choose an empty-headed man for a brief affair, but she is hardly likely to do so for a committed relationship. The women we interviewed are bright, accomplished people, and the young men they love bring an amazing degree of experience, knowledge, and talent to the relationship, amazing for their years. So often women have told us, "He seems so much older than his age," or "He has lived more in five years than I have in ten."

A young man who is on an accelerated time track has much to share with his older partner. A thirty-eight-year-old magazine editor talks about her twenty-nine-year-old artist husband. "He opened up a whole new world to me — a visual world. Because he is an artist, he taught me to pay attention to visual details. As a successful woman living alone, I thought I'd never find a man I could live with. My experience had been that I would have to give up my work — my self even — in order to be loved. Eric taught me I could be in a committed relationship without such a loss."

Young men are excellent teachers of how to enjoy, with the emphasis on joy. Liz Stefano says that Paul has taught her to follow her dreams. Paul's natural spontaneity is part of what helps him constantly support her when she has a new idea. His response is "Great, do it." With his encouragement she takes more chances. Each time she has learned that it is worthwhile to follow her dreams. Paul has always known about following dreams, but Liz is new at daring to live.

Simone, forty-four, describes her friend Robert, twenty, as unusually mature for his age. When Robert was seven, his father died. From that time on, Robert had to look after his two younger sisters while his mother went to work. Simone feels that this experience accounts for Robert's precocious maturity. They met through friends in Paris, although Simone lives in London. Robert took to coming over to visit frequently.

They would sit and talk until two or three in the morning, but it took several months before Simone realized there was a sexual attraction between them. By that time they were quite intimate friends. Simone found Robert's conversation extremely interesting. He talked about his life; she talked about hers. Robert is a free-lance photo-journalist. He introduced Simone to rock music, Zen, and the fascination of photography.

Robert has a flair for fashion and has been delighted in being involved in the finer points of dressing Simone. "Push the sleeves of your blouse up," he says to her. "You must wear your collar so . . . that's how it becomes you." He plays with her hair style and shows her how to get the right look with her fingers instead of a comb. "After twenty years in England, I think I had become a bit dowdy," Simone told us. "Robert put me back together."

Neither Robert nor Simone has any money. What little they have they share. Robert taught Simone how to get along on practically nothing. For Simone, this was a new and valuable skill, since her divorce had left her with very little money. Robert knows how to accept what is and seems not to care about material things he does not have. He owns two pairs of blue jeans, a couple of shirts, and a white Yves St. Laurent scarf. According to Simone, if Robert wore his good boots and his St. Laurent scarf, he could go to tea at Buckingham Palace. He has, as the French say, *l'allure*.

Before a party, he told Simone, "We'd better get the sewing machine out again, I've got another hole in my blue jeans." They patched the jeans from an old pair and then arrived late at the party. Simone says, "I wouldn't dare say to anybody why we were late. Imagine saying, 'Why, we had to put another patch on Robert's britches!' But he walked in there; nobody noticed it. Everyone adored him."

Simone laughs when people say a young man looks to an older woman to teach him. She says, "Either I am an innocent or I am immature; I don't know what to call it. But here I am, forty-four, and he has taught me a lot."

In spite of an age difference of a full generation, Simone never felt significantly older. Most of the time, Robert seemed older than she.

Although there are a number of developmental differences between older women and younger men, there are some surprising similarities. The main differences are obvious. The women have spent more years as adults than the men have; they are that much more experienced in social skills, in caretaking, perhaps even in the working world. In addition, generational differences affect tastes in music, marijuana use, diet, clothing styles, and even politics. Furthermore, men and women are expected to devote themselves to entirely different occupations. He is supposed to earn money; she must keep house. But within this role obligation lies the factor that can easily place an older woman and a younger man at some very similar adult developmental stages. As this kind of couple gets to know each other, they often discover that they are sharing almost identical life experiences despite the age discrepancy.

The male in his twenties is often just beginning to feel himself as an adult in the world. Often the female in older woman/younger man relationships, after spending the major part of her previous adult life in childraising and homemaking, is ready to embark on a full-time career. The younger man and many older women are both developing genuine autonomy for the first time in their lives. Susan Howard talks about this similarity:

"When I was going through my divorce, I felt that my life had exploded. After the debris had settled, I picked my way through the remains trying to figure out what to salvage. At first I was very lost without the comfortable framework of marriage, and then I realized that for the first time in my life, I didn't have any parent figure telling me what to do. I was on my own, finally, at forty-one, scared to death and, simultaneously, loving my personal autonomy. Peter, too, was just beginning to stand on his own two feet, in his working life and in finding his own identity. We were experiencing the same phase of growth and clinging to each other for comfort."

Some younger man/older woman couples have just emerged from a major portion of their formal education. More older women then ever before are going back to school; they are open to new ideas. The younger men are still involved with intellectual and social changes; some are still in college. Both are excited about the challenge of proving themselves in the world. They share a sense of newness and each understands what the other is experiencing. They have attitudes toward life that characterize beginnings: they both feel joy, curiosity, eagerness, energy, excitement. They also feel fear of the unknown. For each one a previous belief system has just been shattered; his childhood concept of how life should be and her years of a traditional marriage have come to an end. In dealing with each other's fears, they generate mutual support, which leads to a greater trust.

The similarity of developmental levels of growth brings about a sharing of life's experiences. This tends to eliminate putting either partner in a one-down position. In a situation where traditional sex roles are largely unimportant, where each person is seeking a balance, the relationship is more peaceful and more nourishing.

Nevertheless, in relationships where either the man or woman is much older than the spouse, family therapists often predict failure. There are many kinds of stress that can affect the well-being of a relationship. One form of stress can be attributed to too great a difference in age. If the partners are of different generations, the gaps in individual outlook may be too difficult to bridge. In addition, many counselors point out that differences in racial, religious, economic, or educational background can cumulatively produce enough stress to destroy the relationship. In the case of the older woman/younger man relationship, there is no question that the combination of age differences and social disapproval could make it very hard for the relationship to survive.

In our clinical practices we have looked at the successful relationships in which the partners come from very different backgrounds, in order to see what qualities make these relationships work. Couples with very dissimilar life experiences, as in different ethnic or religious upbringings, unify their relationship through mutual value systems and life goals. The two people see the world in the same way. Their shared vision of how things are seems to have more to do with intrinsic personality characteristics than with the environment in which each one was raised. The commonality of couples with a ten- or twenty-year age difference is based on a feeling of kinship, the sense of finding an appreciative and understanding friend in an indifferent world.

Strangely enough, it can be the very differences in generational outlook that help to solidify the relationship. From the start, each person sees him- or herself as different from the other in age and experience. Each regards the other as a separate person. The partnership is built on appreciation of one another as individuals, rather than on a shared background. The identity of each person is supported instead of the two being merged. Individuality within the relationship is easier to maintain.

When we investigate the problems of a couple complaining

about the emptiness of their relationship, we often find a turmoil of individual differences carefully concealed beneath a placid facade of unity. Because of the similarities in their backgrounds, both assumed that the kinds of problems that grow from the basic differences of any two human beings would never occur in their relationship. In addition, people change over the years. At best, adaptation to the changes is worked out by the couple, and the relationship goes on, enriched by the couple's ability to overcome problems. In many cases, however, because of the initial similarity of age and background, the couple never developed methods of working out the differences that would, sooner or later, naturally arise.

A general principle of relationships is that two people in a long-lasting marriage must find productive ways to resolve differences. When two people initially have a lot in common, they tend to take for granted agreement with each other on most issues. They are able to avoid dealing with differences for a longer period of time than can a couple with divergent backgrounds. The problems then go underground and can, over the years, erode the foundations of the marriage.

It is true that too many differences can be a constant source of irritation, leading gradually to the dissolution of a relationship. But equally important to bonding is the opportunity to work out differences, to solve problems, to maintain separate identities within the structure of the relationship. Without this, the marriage will not have the flexibility to survive misfortune or change, since flexibility develops largely by dealing with acknowledged differences.

In the older woman/younger man relationship the partners must immediately begin to work on accepting and resolving differences. Differences in age and life experiences have to be worked out as part of the couple's life-style. Some of the issues that arise don't necessarily affect the day-to-day life of the couple, but they are bound to make some of their points of reference very odd.

Susan Howard discussed the disorientation caused by a fifteen-year age difference. "Once when Peter and I were talking we realized that when I gave birth to my first child, Peter was only nine years old. We both found it very strange that I had become a mother at the same time that he was learning to multiply. Then we discovered that when he was six years old the high point of his day was watching the Howdy Doody Show on television. At the time that show was on the air, I was working at NBC and had just become engaged to be married. When things like this come up in our conversation we sometimes look at each other as if we were creatures from another planet. There is no question that we grew up in different times. Peter never heard of Deanna Durbin, and the Second World War is something he learned about from history books. It's weird, but it's also interesting. This kind of thing is a constant reminder that we are two separate people."

Some people feel uncomfortable when faced with another person's total ignorance of familiar points of reference. Taste in popular music, for instance, is absolutely determined by generation. Liz Stefano says about Paul, "He doesn't just listen to music. He's inside it. I can't even understand most of the words on records like the Rolling Stones. Paul knows every single word; I can't figure out how he ever heard them."

A certain amount of individual differences helps to keep a relationship interesting. Being aware of the other partner as essentially different keeps the couple on their toes working out the relationship. Acceptance of differences stabilizes the partnership.

However, psychotherapist Sheldon B. Kopp says, "Like it or not, these same differences between spouses are both the strengths of a good marriage and the hazards of a bad one."[2]

How might differences between older women and younger men be a hazard? An example could be a relationship in which the older woman has her work life well established while the younger man has not. She may fear his becoming dependent; he may be anxious about his self-esteem and jealous of her accomplishments.

One younger man said that it irritated him that his older wife had her life so well under control. "That means that we can't stumble together," he complained. "Sometimes I feel deprived of the chance to stumble with her the way my ex-wife and I did, even though we ended up stumbling right into the divorce court."

Through the marvelous magnifying glass of hindsight we can see the jealousy, competitiveness, and resentment in thirty-year-old Sean's interview remarks. After seven years together, Sean and his wife, Claire, thirty-eight, have separated. From the beginning of their relationship Sean was irritated by the different levels of experience. The tone of his feelings comes through in these comments: "She's experienced a lot of things that I haven't. That was one problem for us from the beginning. Claire had previously been married for fifteen years. Before I lived with her, my laundry got done when I ran out of underwear, not every day. Everything didn't have to be so well organized. All these housekeeping things she did were part of her life with her ex-husband. Obviously, as small as they feel, they were important because they kept reminding me of the experiences that Claire had already gone through." In Claire's case, maturity had brought a strong sense of self-discipline. Claire's ability to organize and carry through often made Sean feel inadequate.

We asked Sean if Claire's business success had been threatening to him. He said, "I can't believe how much money she makes. It blows my mind that she has done it in such a short amount of time. She did it so easily as compared to me. I feel like I've been knocking my head against the wall for too long.

"It also bothers me that she's so independent. She brings in most of the money right now. We've signed a financial agreement that I believe has hurt our relationship. . . . I don't feel I have any type of control."

Sean told us that the first years of his relationship with Claire were the best he had ever had. Something about their relationship allowed him to make changes in himself that he had never dreamed he would permit. At the same time, both the changes in himself and Claire's level of experience frightened him. In addition, the financial agreement he had signed was one he never felt comfortable with. Sooner or later, anyone who agrees to a contract he or she doesn't really want will end up feeling resentful. What had happened was that before they were married, Sean and Claire signed an agreement specifying that they would each pay the same amount for mutual expenses. Shortly after their marriage, Claire began to earn considerably more than Sean. Sean wanted Claire to contribute more money than he, because she had more income. Claire refused. As she put it, "It's the first time in my life that I've had anything of my own, and I don't feel like sharing any more than I already have."

Sean's resentment toward Claire grew until he gradually withdrew from the relationship.

When a couple reacts as Sean and Claire did to a difference about sharing, there is a good chance that the disagreement symbolizes greater underlying issues. For example, Sean might be feeling, "If you really loved me you'd be glad to make my life financially easier," or, "If you get to keep more money, then you'll be more powerful than I am." Claire's behavior might be saying, "The men in my life have kept me financially dependent. If I share my money with you I'll end up the way I was before — powerless. That is never going to happen again."

This kind of conflict is a struggle over power and definitions of love. It goes much deeper than a simple disagreement about who is giving what amount for shared expenses. The rejection implied in each one's behavior toward the other, if unresolved, will eventually destroy the relationship as it did with Sean and Claire.

Generally, people who are older have more life experience than those who are younger. A woman who has been through a previous marriage and has raised children may become impatient with a man's not knowing at twenty-eight what she knows as a result of living ten years longer. Liz Stefano told us how hard it is for her to stay out of Paul's struggle to find a new career. While she is only two years into her new profession, at her age she is certain about wanting a successful psychology practice. Step by step she works toward her goal.

Paul Stefano, who has many talents, is unsure about his direction. He changes his mind a lot. He gets discouraged when he thinks he might get stuck in his secure but unchallenging job. Liz says she knows he must go through this process at his own pace as part of going through life. Sometimes it irritates her that he doesn't know what he really wants. Then she remembers that when she was twenty-eight it hadn't even occurred to her that she wanted to be a psychologist. She tries to hold her tongue and empathize. She doesn't always succeed in doing so.

Older women who accept this difference in experience level will have a better chance at making the relationship work. Such a woman learns to separate herself from the younger man's growing up process. She learns to become a friendly listener and encourage the younger man not to avoid the struggles of adult development.

When older women/younger men couples work and play

in vastly different worlds, they face the difficult task of blending the two. Several spouses had a hard time mixing in the other spouse's social milieu.

Kelly, thirty-nine, and Seth, thirty-one, still argue about why Seth does not fit into Kelly's social circle. She is a film producer. Her friends are show-business types, successful and usually older than Seth, who is just beginning to practice law. During their interview with us they argued about the source and meaning of their problem. Early in the relationship Seth would go to parties with Kelly, and in his usual feisty, abrasive way, he would alienate Kelly's friends. He was not interested in learning social tact, and this upset Kelly. He blamed her friends for rejecting him because he wasn't like them; Kelly blamed his age. She believed there were things he couldn't understand because he was younger than she. He felt strongly that it was just a personality conflict. They did agree on the fact that they don't like the same people.

Eight years later the problem continues, but Seth has toned down his behavior; he is feeling more secure because of his own accomplishments. But in our observation, Kelly and Seth primarily relate through argument; the style of their marriage seems to be an agreement to disagree.

A variety of choices of life-style are common in older woman/younger man couples. When Susan Howard and Peter Levin met, Peter was just emerging from the counterculture, complete with ponytail, scraggly beard, and granny glasses. Susan was an instructor in criminology at a community college, where her particular students were primarily police officers and many of her colleagues were former police officers. Not only did these colleagues look somewhat askance at Peter, but Peter's friends tended to be deeply suspicious of anyone who had anything to do with cops. Peter had experienced the police during Vietnam demonstrations. When he met Susan she was in the thick of empathizing with the law enforcement position. On the surface they seemed to be the unlikeliest couple in the world. But the external differences bothered other people more than they bothered Peter and Susan. They were largely oblivious to what anyone else might think about them.

They began to synthesize their life-styles. Susan and Peter agreed to disagree about politics. They gradually introduced one another to the various groups of friends. They lost some friends, but in most cases each was accepted. Susan and Peter worked hard to like and be liked by one another's friends, since both realized that the integration of friendships was essential to the success of their relationship. They still have a lot of philosophical arguments about every subject in the world. They probably always will. Like Kelly and Seth, Susan and Peter are both pleased to have a life partner who is a strong fighter.

Even though there are differences to be reconciled, the older woman and the younger man do contribute different complementary qualities to each other. He gives youth, idealism, fun, and enthusiasm. She gives stability that is built upon self-knowledge, experience in life, independence, and patience. Both of them give friendship, support, appreciation, an ego boost, role flexibility, and an opportunity for growth. Each teaches the other. In addition, many of these couples are at similar stages of adult development in their educational levels and in their careers. Often they are sharing the process of experiencing life on their own terms for the first time.

Alvin Toffler, in *Future Shock*, predicted there would be more and more relationships between different-age partners in the future. "What will count," says Toffler, "will not be chronological age but complementary values and interests, and above all, the level of personal development. To put it another way, partners will be interested not in age but in stage."[3]

12 ·

THE FUTURE IS NOW

THE MAJOR QUESTION ABOUT AN OLDER WOMAN/ younger man relationship is always "Will it last?" Everyone wants to know the answer. But no one does. Suppose we said statistics show that older woman/younger man couples can outlast all others. Would we be believed? We think not. The question "Will it last?" is asked seriously; yet it is more a statement of doubt than a question. At this time there are no long-term statistical studies comparing the duration of older woman/younger man relationships to other relationships. Therefore, we are not able to answer the question with statistical data. However, we can look at the experiences of several people for whom the future is now. They can tell us what happened to them.

Francine is an elegant, wealthy woman in her seventies. She was widowed at thirty-eight. When she was fifty she fell in love with Jason, who was thirty-five. They married and for twenty years Jason devoted himself to Francine's happiness and comfort. At fifty-five Jason fell in love with a woman his own age. He and Francine were divorced and Francine, now seventy years old, faced the devastating loss of her husband. We asked her if she had any regrets. She replied, "I had twenty wonderful years. I only regret that my marriage did not go on longer."

There are many ways to interpret Francine's experience. Since her husband left her, we could say, "Beware a younger man, for he will leave you when you are old." This marriage did not last forever. But is a happy twenty-year marriage a failure merely because it ended? Even though Francine now faces the last years of her life without Jason, does that nullify the previous twenty years?

After thirty years of marriage, Ted Connally, a fifty-eight-year-old retired police officer, is building a dream house for his wife, Carol, sixty-eight. He is an electrician now and in his spare time he spends long hours constructing his gift of love for Carol. Ted is anxious to finish the house soon because Carol recently had a serious heart attack. Carol has other ailments as well, but she had made up her mind that she is going to have at least ten years in her beautiful new home.

Ted and Carol live in a small town in Montana. Most of their friends don't know that Carol is older because she has always looked so young and because Ted and Carol keep the information private. For example, if they meet a couple where the man is sixty-five and the woman is fifty-five, Ted will say, "Oh, you folks are about our age," and not bother to explain further.

Ted's conservative, old-country family, who live in the East, have never known Carol's age. In fact, Ted himself was surprised when he found out that she was ten years his senior. They had been dating for eight months when Carol's daughter by a first marriage made a remark which placed Carol's age. Ted tried to get Carol to marry him for several years, but Carol kept turning him down because of the age difference. Finally she agreed to the marriage. Today Carol says she's sorry she wasted those years. Four years after they were married, Carol, at the age of forty-two, gave birth to her second child.

Carol has never worried about losing Ted to another woman. "Ted," Carol told us, "is a man with an honest and firm set of morals." Although his life as a bachelor was a bit wild, when he met Carol he began to change and to focus his life around her family. Ted is handsome, kind, and responsible; for those reasons women are attracted to him. "But," Carol says, "Ted is also faithful and devoted to me. He often tells me, 'I make the living and you make the living worthwhile.' "

The story of Ted and Carol is utterly romantic. After thirty years they are still in love. Now, Carol's illness threatens their life together. Her heart attack made Ted realize he could lose her. We asked what their advice would be to other older woman/younger man couples. Ted said, "Don't keep bringing the age difference up all the time." And Carol added, "Keep your sex life going. I enjoy making love. The worst part of having had the heart attack is that it has caused us to have less frequent, briefer lovemaking. Why, we only make love once a week now. But Ted says when the house is done we'll christen every single room together."

The Connallys have not been split up by fears about older woman/younger man relationships. They have kept their marriage in good health for thirty years. So far, they have dealt successfully with the kinds of problems that older woman/younger man couples worry about facing, concern about the woman being older, bearing a child after the age of forty, and debilitating illness.

We can predict that older woman/younger man pairs will face certain problems in old age. For instance, a long and debilitating illness can be a serious problem. An older woman may die earlier than her younger husband, especially when the age difference is twenty years or more. This is simply a reverse of the usual situation, where a woman is widowed by a husband the same age. But if the age difference is ten years or less, statistics say that the pair are likely to die at about the same time.

The way problems of old age are handled by the older woman/younger man couple is determined by the attitude of each partner. We are optimistic about the couples we interviewed, because we kept hearing them describe a positive vision of old age. The women, especially, expressed confidence that their old age would be filled with lively activity and new goals. Jenna Trenton, now fifty-four, saw herself in a motorized wheelchair, gambling in Las Vegas. Liz Stefano, presently thirty-eight, told us, "When I'm old I'll be a rowdy typo, full of life and adventure. I'll be naughty, very naughty. I'll keep learning new things. I'll hang out with young people. Paul and I will be white-haired motorcyclists buzzing happily down the freeways with the other weekend riders."

Doug and Peggy Randall have already begun to discuss plans for their retirement. Doug, thirty-six, and Peggy, forty-nine, have been married eight years. Doug is a minister and Peggy shares her dedication to his work. Doug said, "If we wait till I'm sixty-five to retire, chances are we might not have time to enjoy our retirement years together." Peggy added, "So many men die between sixty-five and seventy who never were able to enjoy their retirement. Maybe we'll retire for the next ten years and then go back to work." The Randalls are creating solutions to the problems their age difference brings up. They have an optimistic, flexible approach to the future.

The question "Will it last?" might also translate to "Is marriage to an older woman or a younger man a big gamble with the odds stacked against us?" We understand how this question can worry people. But because we are family therapists we know that all relationships are risky. Couples with everything in their favor break up. Couples who are passionately in love break up. Unlikely couples stay together. Risk is a given factor for all couples. No one, absolutely no one, can predict if a relationship will last. A couple's fate is determined largely by the behavior and decisions of the couple themselves.

Doris and Hal have been married for eighteen years. They met when Doris was forty-two and Hal was thirty-one. Doris had been married once before. Slender, tanned, and silver-haired, Doris does not remotely look her sixty years. Hal is poised and well groomed, every inch the successful executive. Their friends see them as a couple who are totally devoted to one another. They have rarely done anything or gone anywhere without each other. Doris is articulate but distraught as she tells us about an event that may have destroyed their idyllic marriage. "I still find it hard to believe," she says. The set of her jaw is firm but her hands clench and unclench in mute despair. "I don't know what could have gone wrong. We had such a perfect marriage." Hal sits quietly accepting the torrent of anguish that Doris pours out. Recently he told Doris that for the last six months, he has been having an affair. "I don't understand it either," he mutters. "I love Doris more than anyone in the world. Why did I do it? I never wanted to hurt her."

Well, let's look at the situation. Hal's lover was a few years younger than himself. But Hal felt no particular pride about the affair. He was as confused about his behavior as his wife was. Was Hal having an affair because he wanted a younger woman? Doris was concerned about that possibility. However, Hal's affair had nothing to do with the prophecy that the younger man is bound to leave his older wife. The real issue for Hal and Doris was a problem with their relationship.

While Doris told us more about their marriage, Hal shifted around in his chair, but said nothing. Patterns of their interaction began to emerge. Hal had always been an easygoing kind of guy, Doris explained, sweet, playful, and rather indecisive in their personal relationship. It was difficult to get a yes or no answer out of him. Had either one of them gone through any great changes over the years?

"No," Doris said, "that's what I find so hard to understand. Everything has always been pretty much the same."

"Well, that's not quite true," Hal interrupted. "In the years I've been with Doris, I've become very successful. Before I married her, I wasn't much of anything. Doris believed in me. She supported me, helped me, and encouraged me. I have a lot more self-confidence today than I ever did. That's all the more reason why I don't understand why I hurt her like this."

The interaction between Doris and Hal indicated that over the years Hal had changed, but Doris had refused to acknowledge that a change had taken place. She still treated him the way she had twenty years earlier. When one partner in a marriage, after eighteen years, suddenly manifests behavior utterly unlike his or her previous actions, such as having an affair out of the blue, it is usually an attempt to get the other partner's attention. It is somewhat akin to hitting the proverbial stubborn mule between the eyes with a two-by-four in order to get his attention and is just as violently painful as that act implies. Yet, basically, that seemed to be the purpose behind Hal's sexual fling. A quiet man and rather passive, he simply wasn't able to get past Doris's expert way with words, her cogent arguments and eminent reasonableness. Hal's actions were such that Doris was sure to discover the affair. When she finally did, Hal freely admitted the affair and told her he would be willing to end it. His message was given and received and the reason for the affair was over.

When one partner in a marriage tells the other of an infidelity, it takes a long time for the other partner's feeling of betrayal, anger, and sorrow to diminish. And the relationship, if it goes on at all, is forever changed. Doris will never take Hal quite as much for granted anymore, but her feeling that everything she believed about the relationship has changed may not allow her to continue the marriage. Experiencing a trauma of this magnitude is hardly the most efficient way for normal changes to take place in a marriage. Often the marriage does not survive this kind of announcement of a change.

Change is inevitable. It is probably the only thing in life that is absolutely certain to happen. In any given relationship the individual partners involved are changing and growing all of the time. What does not grow, dies. Periodically, the structure of a marriage has to be rearranged to suit the changes of the individual partners. Agreements that were appropriate in the first year of marriage may no longer be workable after two years, seven years, twelve years, or twenty years. At each of these points assessments may have to be made and new agreements reached. Unusual behavior on the part of one or both partners, such as an outside sexual liaison, is often the signal that a change is overdue.

Doris and Hal, in an older woman/younger man marriage, are not exempt from the problems that affect all long-term relationships. For the last three years Doris had been aware that something was amiss but had not wanted to look closely at it or to listen to what Hal was trying to tell her about himself. Hal is not a particularly assertive person. His unwillingness to hurt Doris, to tell her something about his changing needs that might have been painful for her to hear, has resulted in her being unbelievably hurt by the way that the news finally exploded. Years of trust have been destroyed. Only the goodwill garnered from the previous eighteen years plus the solid determination to go on from here will rebuild the marriage. There is no guarantee that a marriage can heal from such a trauma. Indeed there is no guarantee that any marriage, older woman/younger man or other, can survive the internal and external stresses that beset all marriages.

However, if there are common denominators to the successful older woman/younger man relationship, they are (1) an unusual willingness to take risks, (2) assertiveness as acceptable, even necessary, behavior in both sexes, and (3) mutual emotional supportiveness. These characteristics appear repeatedly in the biographies of historical persons committed to older woman/younger man relationships. This may also be the only pertinent data we have about the longevity of these relationships, since all of our interviewees are still living.

For instance, the prophet Muhammad, founder of the Islamic religion, was married for twenty-five years to a widow who was fifteen years older than he. Khadija, who was a wealthy and accomplished woman, saw in the young Muhammad a person of rare dignity and responsibility who was worthy of her hand in marriage. During the years of their marriage Muhammad's older wife bore him five children. Khadija was thirty-five when they were married and died at the age of fifty. Muhammad considered the union a blessed one, full of affection and great mutual respect.

Aurore Dupin, Baroness Dudevant, more familiarly known as George Sand, had a series of long-term relationships with men who were younger than she. At thirty-two, Sand fell in love with twenty-six-year-old Frédéric Chopin. They were lovers for nine years. At forty-five, Sand began a relationship with Alexandre Manceau, thirty-two, who lived with her until he died seventeen years later. And scattered through the years, there were other men with whom she formed temporary liaisons and lifetime friendships. To each lover, she was friend and confidante as well as mistress. At times she was the sole financial support for herself, her current lover, and a huge extended family. Her lovers, in turn, gave her help with her family problems, extensive emotional and physical care as well as a broad backing of intellectual stimulation and acceptance.

George Sand anticipated the advent of expanded sex roles with her decision to define her way of life by her own standards. She incorporated both masculine and feminine types of behavior as part of her style of living and in so doing repeatedly risked social ostracism. George Sand's determination to extend the conventional female role allotted to her was nowhere so explicitly stated as in the Russian writer Turgenev's comment to her old friend Flaubert after her death. "What a good man she was," Turgenev wrote, "and what a kind woman!"[1]

In 1846, the poet Elizabeth Barrett married a fellow poet, Robert Browning. She was forty years old at the time and he was thirty-six. Elizabeth Barrett had been an invalid most of her life. Her doctors gave her less than a year to live if she insisted on risking her fragile health on the rigors of married life. Their prognosis was wrong. Elizabeth and Robert Browning traveled, wrote, and published their poetry and shared a gratifying marriage, including the birth of a son when Elizabeth was forty-five, until her death in 1859. A willingness to take risks and an acceptance of each other as peer professionals characterized Elizabeth Barrett's relationship with Robert Browning.

At the age of thirty-three, Benjamin Disraeli married Mary Anne Lewis, a forty-five-year-old widow. Rumor had it that Disraeli married his older wife for her money, but the memoirs of their friends describe them as a devoted and singularly happy couple. When Disraeli died, his will directed that he not be buried with the public ceremony that was due a former prime minister of England. He chose instead to be laid to rest quietly beside his beloved wife of thirty years.

Lady Randolph Churchill was forty-three when she fell in love with twenty-one-year-old George Cornwallis-West, who was the same age as her son Winston. Their love affair created a scandal in Victorian England and alienated most of Jennie Churchill's closest friends, including Albert Edward, Prince of Wales. Her biographer, Ralph G. Martin, stated, "British society was more than astonished. It was incensed."[2] Yet, two years later the couple were married. And although her young husband was described as "improvident and callow,"[3] the marriage lasted for fifteen years. Jennie's husband divorced her to marry another woman older than he, and Jennie, for a time, was despondent. But her beauty and charm at sixty were still undiminished. Her nephew, Shane Leslie, said of her, "she could have married young men until she was a hundred."[4] He was shortly proved right. When Jennie was sixty-four, she married Montagu Porch, forty-one. Jennie did not consider that it might be an unsuitable match. "He has a future and I have a past," she said to a friend, "so we should be all right."[5]

The historical celebrities we have mentioned all have personality characteristics in common with their contemporary counterparts in older woman / younger man relationships. They possessed a willingness to risk a nonconforming relationship, and the ability to assert themselves. The patterns of past relationships of older women and younger men also closely resemble those that occur today. The emphasis on mutual respect, on a peer relationship, was significant. The relative longevity of these relationships was similar as well; some were lifetime marriages and some ended in divorce. Certain older woman / younger man couples lived together for a period of years and then moved on.

People who combine nonconforming behavior with a desire to live self-determined lives are exemplified in a movie that came out about ten years ago and has become something of a cult film. The movie is *Harold and Maude*. It tells the story of miserably unhappy Harold, a young man obsessed with death. In an unsuccessful attempt to rebel against his hyperconforming mother, he routinely initiates a series of insanely hilarious suicide attempts. One of his great passions is attending funerals. One rainy afternoon, while he is indulging in this bleak pastime, he meets Maude, an eighty-year-old woman who shares his pleasure in funerals. However, she is neither miserable nor suicidal. On the contrary, Maude is a person as singlemindedly devoted to living as Harold is concentrated on dying. Death, to her, is simply a natural part of living, a logical ending that persons may choose when they feel they have drunk their fill of life. Maude herself is an extremely unorthodox human being who has spent her life doing only what she has chosen to do and loving every minute of it.

They fall in love and, with Maude as his guide, Harold begins to learn how to live. At the end of the movie, Maude chooses to die as she has lived: on her own terms, at her own time, in her own way. She bequeaths to Harold the legacy of his own life, to be lived on his own terms and not by somebody else's standards.

The indomitable Maude was played by Ruth Gordon, a first lady of the American theatre, who has lived her entire life with the same stubborn determination exhibited by the character she portrays in *Harold and Maude*. Miss Gordon is eighty-three years old. In her autobiography, *Myself among Others*, published in 1971, she wrote about her husband, writer-director Garson Kanin, "Twenty-eight years ago this December, I started getting it right when I married the best man in the world. And after twenty-eight years he's still the best man."[6]

The Kanins were married when Miss Gordon was forty-six and Mr. Kanin was thirty. In addition to their individual careers, they collaborated as a writing team on such successful screenplays as *Adam's Rib*, *A Double Life*, and *Pat and Mike*. After thirty-six years of marriage Garson Kanin talks about Ruth Gordon at eighty-two in his latest book, *It Takes a Long Time to Become Young*: "If there is one subject on which I am an expert, it is the subject of Ruth Gordon. I know how she lives and how she works . . . at fifteen, she decided to become an actress — without money, without apparent aptitude, without conventional good looks, without resources. These debits were outweighed by a single credit: determination. . . ."[7]

A certain amount of determination is essential to the successful older woman/younger man relationship. These people who choose such a marriage might do well to pay careful attention to Ruth Gordon's guiding principle in life: "Never give up; and never, under any circumstances, no matter what — *never* face the facts!"[8]

If "facing the facts" means succumbing to conventional pressures and expectations, then Ruth Gordon's motto might have been invented for the older woman/younger man couple. Despite the aura of doubt that surrounds their relationship, older woman/younger man couples go right on settling down to the business of living out their lives with each other.

13 ·

WHAT CAN WE LEARN?

COUPLES OF ALL AGES CAN BENEFIT FROM WHAT older women/younger men couples have learned about creating a workable relationship. The couples we studied produced a number of useful new solutions to the vexing problems of today's and tomorrow's marriages. In times of rapid social change, people experiment with their lives in order to adapt. Some of these experiments work, while others die out. We believe that the older woman/younger man couple is a social phenomenon that will endure, because the relationship seems particularly well suited to withstand the pressures of contemporary life.

The achieving woman is a part of the family of the future. Nearly all women will work and many of those women will gain power, status, and high earning ability. The process has already begun. And, when a woman experiences the benefits of increased educational and economic power she will not continue to accept relationships in which she experiences herself as one-down.

As usual, social change leaps ahead of attitude change, fostering chaos within the couple. In spite of facts to the contrary, men and women continue to hold to the idea that men should be "more than" women.

If men believe their identity is tied up in being "more than" their wives, what will happen to the concept of marriage if women become "equal to" or even "more than" their husbands? And men are not alone. Women, too, believe their men should be somehow more significant than they.

One of the most persistent blocks to success for women is the belief that if they succeed at their careers they will lose their relationships with their husbands and lovers. Women stumble, hesitate, and fall on the road to success because of that powerful belief. Women who work for success without hesitation often ignore the issue of a permanent relationship altogether. They refuse to get seriously involved, hoping to avoid the power and role conflicts. But avoiding relationships is not a solution. And women at the top want to know where they can find appropriate and interested mates.

The key words are *appropriate* and *interested*. Many older women in relationships with younger men say their requirements for a mate are vastly different than in the past. They want a man who will accept a woman as she is, complete with career goals, independence, and equal say in making decisions and bearing responsibilities. Many of today's women no longer need a man for the money and status he provides; they are capable of making their own money and creating their own status. They want a man who is not afraid of a powerful woman; they are unwilling to baby men, to protect men from the reality of a woman's strength in driving toward her own goals.

Therefore, "appropriate," for these women, does not necessarily mean that a man has to have equal or greater achievements. "Appropriate" means a man who is comfortable with a woman who is his equal, or who may accomplish more than he, and "interested," for these women, translates as men who are as committed to the fulfillment of their mates' life goals as they are to their own.

Women over thirty-five say they have a hard time finding mates among their contemporaries, and the older they are the worse it gets. According to census figures there are 14 million women over sixty-five and only 9.5 million men. Seventy-four percent of the men over sixty-five live with their wives. Added to the numbers problem is the fact that middle-aged men frequently choose to marry younger women. Moreover, the brighter, the more successful, and the more assertive a woman is, the less likely it is that she will be appreciated by a man who is her contemporary. And many women over forty find it equally difficult to relate to men their own age. Our female interviewees described older men at various times as "boring," "rigid," "chauvinistic," "competitive," and "controlling."

One forty-six-year-old woman referred to a particular kind of middle-aged man as an "infant tyrant." An infant tyrant to her is a chronologically adult male, usually professionally successful, with the emotional development of a five-year-old. The infant tyrant rages when he does not get his own way. He hears any request for consideration or change as a demand. He takes any disagreement with his beliefs as a severe personal affront. "I'd rather be alone for the rest of my life," this interviewee concluded, "than live with that kind of man."

And where *are* the interested men for older women? Our interviewees report that interested men are nowhere to be found. The woman sales managers, bank executives, lobbyists, law partners, film producers, the women who have everything — intelligence, position, money, and personal attractiveness — often pay the price of being alone. It's not that men aren't attracted to them. It's just that when the relationship comes to a serious stage, the men back off.

Throughout this book we have pointed out how subconscious rules, beliefs, and motivations come into play around the older woman/younger man relationship. Again we want to emphasize that men are put off by women who are their equals because they have been conditioned to believe they must be one-up. Once they realize they will not be one-up in a relationship they back off. Often they marry younger, less successful women in order to retain the one-up position.

A great deal can be learned from older woman/younger man couples about how to solve the problems presented by a marriage in which the woman has equal or greater status than the man. Couples who are the same age and even couples where the man is older must learn to integrate the changing roles of women into a successful marriage. And there are few current models for this change except the older woman/younger man couple.

Couples like Susan Howard and Peter Levin are working out the problems in a different kind of relationship. Susan and Peter have devised a money system in which each contributes an amount in proportion to income earned. More important than the money arrangement are the feelings it brings up. The hardest work for Susan and Peter is to live with the fact that Susan has more money in a world where nearly everyone believes it is wrong for a woman to have "more than." To compensate for the discrepancy, Peter and Susan find ways to equalize their power. They discuss their feelings openly. Susan gives up control quite deliberately over some economic decisions and in certain business negotiations. Susan looks up to Peter in areas where he is more expert than she.

Jenna earns three times the salary of twenty-eight-year-old Barry, yet Barry controls the money. Jenna, at fifty-four, readily admits she has less need to control or compete at this stage of her life. They talk about each other with the greatest admiration, each emphasizing the special assets of the other. Instead of competing, each enhances the other's attributes.

Paul and Liz Stefano bought a house with down-payment money from Liz's previous home. Paul has the steady job that enabled them to get the loan, and for several years he has made a larger proportion of the payments. Essentially, for Liz and Paul economic power is more traditionally balanced than for Susan and Peter and Jenna and Barry.

The older women/younger men couples we interviewed have consciously sought a balance of power. When the balance shifted to the woman, as in Susan and Jenna's cases, each found ways to even out the power.

To begin with, each partner in the older woman/younger man relationship accepts the fact that there are often areas where the woman has more power than the man. They talk openly about how they feel about that fact. If they are comfortable with it, as in the case of a woman physiotherapist who supported her sculptor husband for ten years until his work began to sell, the only problem might be the reactions of outsiders to their arrangement.

The response of others can be a heavy pressure. Even a same-age couple who breaks the "more than" rule must be strong enough, confident enough, and lighthearted enough to face the snide comments of the outside world. The press speculates whether the husband of Margaret Thatcher, the Prime Minister of Great Britain, will "host teas" for her. Jane Byrne, the Mayor of Chicago, is the butt of cruel sexist humor and her husband is included as well.

If a power imbalance is not to their liking, a couple can find ways to correct it. Many men and women we spoke to consciously decided to give financial control over to the other person. Some older women have turned over all money matters to their younger husbands. Certain younger husbands preferred that their wives handle all business affairs.

Consciously working toward a power balance is part of a solution to the power struggle. An even more important component of sharing power is learning to cooperate. Over and over our interviewees talked about mutuality, helping one another reach career goals, and taking turns. Instead of focusing on who has the most influence, they talk about how they can live with their differences, how to negotiate power, and how each respects and supports the opportunities open to the other.

It is paradoxical that this intensively cooperative marriage style is practiced by strong, independent, professionally competitive men and women. It may be that these couples are learning that the qualities that make for success in the working world are not always the qualities that make successful family life.

Both men and women must change in order to make relationships which will accommodate the fact that women's roles are changing. Women must learn not to relinquish power to a man automatically. And men must appreciate the benefits of sharing power. In the words of one younger man, "I grew up around intelligent women . . . we were pretty much equals. I don't feel it's a threat when they are more competent than I am. We have our different areas of competence. . . . It makes me feel good that I am good enough to be with someone who is more competent — that reflects well on me."

Several younger husbands told us they believe they will live longer because they are able to share emotional and financial burdens with their older wives. They believe that men often die years earlier than women because men bear such persistent stress as accomplishers and providers. In addition, traditionally, men have had a more difficult time than women in adapting to changing life situations like retirement. Men in relationships with women who are older think they carry less personal stress; they believe their role flexibility will enable them to do a better job of adapting to life's changing circumstances.

When older women and younger men make a relationship

in which power is shared equally, to the world it looks as if the young man were giving up power. He does not; what he gives up is dominating the relationship and his partner. It is a trade-off in which the young man may gain greater fulfillment and greater supportiveness to assist him in his life. Often male dominance is burdensome, since a man's power in a relationship is largely derived from unending financial and decision-making responsibilities. Giving up the struggle for dominance, sharing power, results in shared responsibility and a shared life. However, negotiating power is a difficult, subtle task for most couples who are the same age.

Our observation is that when the woman is older than the man, her greater age and experience neutralizes the tendency for the man to expect more power and for the woman to try to give up her power to him. The myth that older women invariably dominate young men was definitely not the case in our sampling of committed couples. What we saw was a model for sharing power. Quite accidentally the age difference has assisted the process.

Divorce is another major problem of modern life. Currently, the odds are 50-50 that a couple will divorce. In spite of all our beliefs and myths to the contrary, most marriages are not going to last a lifetime. This means most of us will face the painfully difficult problems of divorce, living alone, remarriage, and stepchildren.

Since older woman/younger man couples face a world that believes their relationship can't possibly last, they must face the issue of breaking up just as they begin the process of their commitment. They can't avoid thinking about it because others are sure to suggest that the younger man will leave the older woman. On top of outsiders' suggestions are the internal fears of the couple themselves, the internalization of society's rules. Facing the possibility that their relationship may end entails building into it coping devices. The older women and younger men maintain a high level of emotional and financial independence. They have an attitude which is expressed in this way: "Nothing is forever. This is good so I will enjoy it as long as I can. I'll do my best to keep it going. Whatever happens, I know I'll be okay."

Liz Stefano's remarks reflect the attitude of many of the women in older women/younger men relationships. "Since the very start of our relationship I have deliberately kept up my independent activities. I go places alone; I spend time with my friends. I have some separate money. At first it was kind of defiant, as though I was saying, 'I don't need you that much.' Later on, when we were secure together, I continued because I enjoy it, because I need some separate life and because it protects me. Economic independence is extremely important to me. It means being able to take care of myself and it means I can choose my man free of financial need."

Economic independence came up a number of times in the women's interviews. Marketing analyst Jennifer Selby told us, "My mother always said a woman should have her own money; she always had her own money. And I've always believed that. As long as I have my own money, I can feel independent in a relationship."

Divorce was common to nearly all of the women we interviewed. That experience taught them the importance of self-sufficiency. Older women, even in their new relationships, keep that independence going.

The younger men we interviewed wanted independent women. Their reasons varied. Jeff Courtney-Fein, thirty, is an artist whose projects take him on frequent trips. He wanted to be with a woman who could accept the separations without trauma. Paul Stefano prefers women who are strong and independent. He says he doesn't want to carry all the responsibilities. He wants to be taken care of part of the time. The remarks of some younger men reflect a shift in attitude away from the traditional, fatherly, responsible, caretaking male role.

Whenever there is abundant divorce, there follow remarriage and the consequent problems of the blended family and stepparenting. The blended family consists of the old family members plus the new family members. Stepparents have little enough knowledge to go on. Negative culture images such as the mean stepmother or the brutal stepfather aren't much help. So the brave stepparent just fumbles along doing his or her best.

We supposed that the younger men we interviewed would be additionally hampered by being close in age to the older woman's children. In fact, the younger man stepfathers make a strong place for themselves in their families, a place that varies according to the needs of that particular family. Where there is a weak, distant, or uninvolved natural father, the young stepfather frequently takes a strong father role. When the natural father is present and involved, the stepfather gives himself the role of loving adult friend.

The younger man, instead of automatically trying to be a parent to children who are not his, simply attempts to find a logical place in the family where he can fit easily. Since he usually shares in the rest of the woman's household tasks, he also involves himself in the care and rearing of her children. The pace of his involvement will depend on a number of factors, the friendliness or resistance of the children, the degree of conflict of new husband and wife over how to raise children, and the confidence of the younger man.

No one assumes that the younger man can move right into the fathering role. So he approaches his stepchildren cautiously, taking nothing for granted. Men who have married same-age wives have learned, often the hard way, that their stepchildren do not automatically accept them into the parenting role either.

The degree and pacing of involvement is the basis on which the new stepparent will be integrated into the family. The gradual approach might be helpful to any adult who is blending into a new family system.

The children in a blended family need the old family and the new family to cooperate. While there is always some jealousy, competition, and resentment, the more the adults concerned can set that aside the better it will be for the children. Of course, cooperation takes time and hard work to achieve. For the Stefanos it took four years to get to the point where the whole blended family could go out to dinner to celebrate Liz Stefano's daughter's junior high graduation. That event was built on a long series of positive conversations and cooperative behavior on both sides.

Older women/younger men couples are better able to cope with the problems attendant upon divorce because of a heightened sense of separateness combined with a willingness to be interdependent. The man and the woman encourage each other's financial and emotional independence. As family therapists, we encourage a healthy independence in relationships as well as the necessary dependence. As human beings we are dependent on each other in the sense that "no man is an island." But as adults we can choose whom we are going to be dependent on, what extent of dependence is acceptable, and when dependence is appropriate. We can negotiate and arrange our dependence.

A child, for instance, is essentially dependent on an adult to meet his or her physical and emotional needs. An adult when ill, despondent, or suffering a loss has those same needs for another's care. But for the adult, the dependence is temporary. In addition, the adult can consciously request the kind of care he or she needs. The result is interdependence, a deliberate movement from dependence, to independence, to interdependence, according to what each individual in the relationship requires at any given time.

The difference between dependence and interdependence is that childish dependence is not conscious; it involves a lot of manipulation and game playing. Interdependence is a conscious state and is expressed by reciprocal love and caring and interest. As one woman told us, "Basically, I'm a strong person but sometimes I'm as frightened as a little child. If I'm upset I want to be held when I cry. I ask for help until I come out of it."

Paradoxically, it is true interdependence that enables couples to depend on one another freely for support. In uncertain times, the interdependent couple has a good chance for survival. Again we see a paradox; people who feel free to break away know they are in a relationship by choice, which increases the odds they will remain.

Future relationships will reflect values and goals quite different from those in the past. Yesterday's marriages were geared chiefly to basic physical survival, in the sense that two people together could better create the wherewithal that would allow life to continue. Survival was reason enough for a marriage to endure. Other values had to be subordinated. But when survival is not an immediate issue, what happens to the institution of marriage?

According to psychologist Abraham Maslow, human beings must be assured of their physical survival before they are in a position to develop further. For instance, Maslow postulates an ascending hierarchy of needs in which physiological needs such as hunger and thirst must be met before a human can turn his or her attention to safety needs, the next level of accomplishment. And only after security against the elements and personal danger has been obtained does a human being reach out for the fulfillment of belonging and love.[1]

Traditionally, the first three levels of Maslow's heirarachy of needs might be all that a couple within a marriage expects to accomplish in a lifetime. In an earlier time, the struggle just to fulfill physiological safety needs often precluded the possibility that there might be more to a marriage than basic survival and a sense of belonging.

However, the circumstances of urban human life have changed for a large segment of society. Both men and women are individually capable of providing food and a place to live for themselves as well as finding friends to love and be loved by. Marriage and family, formerly a place of physical and, sometimes, emotional security, is no longer an essential survival need. And for the first time, the struggle for pure physiological survival can give way to other needs.

In today's world many men and women have placed an enormous emphasis on Maslow's fourth level of development, the desire to achieve self-esteem and the esteem of others.[2] In a marriage this value has become primary. In a traditional marriage, esteem is given by each partner to the other for fulfilling the allotted male and female sex roles that would allow the family to survive. A woman who is a good homemaker can feel high self-esteem. Her husband and others will admire her accomplishments. A man who is a good provider can feel good about his role. But changing roles have created confusion about how to gain esteem in a relationship. Couples are thrashing about attempting to adapt to the changes. Many relationships are hurt or destroyed in the process.

We need a new model. When simple survival ceases to be the issue, each partner looks for other arenas in which to gain the esteem essential to personal development. The role expansion we have seen in the older woman/younger man marriage provides a basis for the two human beings involved in a committed relationship to reach this level of development.

Barbara Courtney-Fein is not able to gain self-esteem by playing the traditional sex role. Just as most men look to work for satisfaction, so does Barbara. A husband who expected her to take care of him would find her lacking. The marriage she has made reflects her needs and the needs of her husband, Jeff. Jeff thinks Barbara's writing success is bolstered by his admiration, encouragement, and patience. Yet Jeff is free to pursue his photographic projects with Barbara's total support. Each has backed the other as an individual; each appreciates the assets of the other. Jeff does all the cooking; Barbara shops and cleans up. Their mutual support even goes as far as their being willing to spend long times apart when necessary. Jeff and Barbara have mutual friends as well as separate sets of friends. If they invite a member of a couple to dinner they extend the invitation to both or to either. This behavior reflects a style of marriage that assumes a couple is also two separate individuals.

Barbara and Jeff work their life-style around the demands of each person's career and life goals. Each of them enhances the other's life. There is a conscious down-playing of competitiveness, jealousy, and possessiveness. Instead they focus on cooperation, compatibility, and the desire to give each other room to live.

When self and mutual esteem are encouraged, marriage enhances the possibility of each partner's moving on to the final level of human development, the stage Maslow calls self-actualization. Maslow's portrayals of self-actualized people closely parallels the descriptions of the individuals in older women/younger men relationships. He writes, ". . . healthy people have sufficiently gratified their basic needs for safety, belongingness, love, respect and self-esteem so that they are motivated primarily by trends to self-actualization (defined as ongoing actualization of potentialities, capacities and talents, as fulfillment of mission . . . and acceptance of the person's own intrinsic nature . . .)."[3]

Maslow concluded that self-actualized people have noticeable characteristics. Among others he lists:

1. Superior perception of reality,
2. Increase in problem-centering,
3. Increased autonomy, and resistance to enculturation,
4. Greater freshness of appreciation, and richness of emotional reaction,
5. Improved interpersonal relations,
6. Greatly increased creativeness.[4]

Self-actualization is the fulfillment of the ultimate potential of an individual human being, the realization of a man's or woman's life goals, dreams, and ideals. It is a process and not a state of being. Many of our interviewees contrasted their current behavior with past behavior, pointing especially to their ability to appreciate what would have threatened them at another time. One woman said, "The other night we had friends over and we didn't know they were staying for dinner. There was nothing in the kitchen of any value that I could see. Within thirty minutes, my husband put out this beautiful meal. I said, 'Where did that food come from? There's nothing in the refrigerator.' It was not only visually beautiful, it was delicious. In the past I would have panicked because I would have felt obligated but not known how to get it together myself. I sat there and felt really proud of him. I can remember when I would have sat there and said, 'Damn it, I can't do that.' So that's new for me. And along those lines I guess there are other things that I don't feel competitive about that I would have before in a relationship."

Susan Howard and Peter Levin think that they can take on more work as individuals because they have become "interchangeable." Peter says, "Each day we divide up the tasks according to who wants to do what and how we feel. A typical day might include: go to the bank, handle the crisis call of one of the kids, have the upholstery cleaned, buy some wineglasses, or attend a business meeting with a lawyer. Neither of us has all the responsibility. It seems we have more energy for ourselves and our goals by being flexible about who does what." The sharing of power growing out of the role-expanded marriage creates a rich environment for self-actualization.

Throughout this discussion the theme of role flexibility has come up many times. The single most common trait exhibited by older women/younger men couples is sex-role flexibility. It is absolutely not an exchange of sex-related roles; rather it is an expansion of those roles for each person in the relationship. Such flexibility enables older women and younger men to vary their roles according to the needs of their marriage.

Couples who go beyond traditionally allotted sex role tasks can have more flexible relationships. Whatever opportunities or mishaps life brings will be met with an easier adaptation if each person is able to play alternative roles and capably carry out different kinds of tasks. Older women/younger men couples are frequently made up of androgynous individuals; women who lead, assert, and decide as well as nurture and look good, men who express feelings, take care of the home and kids as well as make decisions and make money.

In times past, men and women who enjoyed activities allotted to their opposite sex were thought to be maladjusted. Non-macho men were labeled sissy. Professionally competent women were called emasculators. Outspoken women who had ambitions but no way to fulfill those goals often turned into nagging harridans, driving their husbands on to greater and greater achievements and sometimes to their deaths. Role expansion brings to individuals who have lived as misfits acceptance and an alternative to shrewish behavior.

Another beneficial side effect of sex-role expansion is that each person fully understands the work and domestic problems of the other. Traditional marriages many times produce a worker and a housewife who have little understanding of one another's lives. Housewives resent their husbands' preoccupation with work and husbands resent their wives' socalled easy lives, each complaining of a lack of support. Where there is sex-role expansion, each person understands the other's pressures. It is an understanding that comes from experience and not from a leap of imagination.

Most of the older woman/younger man couples we interviewed created relationships that also allowed each individual to function without the other. Instead of trying to make the other feel guilty for not doing his or her proper tasks, the husband or the wife would step in and take over. When Paul Stefano works eight days straight, twelve hours a day, Liz Stefano takes over all other responsibilities, finances, errands, meals, foot rubbing, and trashcans. When Liz works long hours or goes on work trips, Paul takes over in the same way, meals, the home, chauffeuring their child, and laundry. They tell us that if both had to work overtime at the same time, they would put their heads together and figure out a solution.

Liz and Paul have made a marriage of flexible cooperation that provides full support for their career goals. We call this relationship style a third option. As long as there are only two choices, the woman as backup to the man or the man as backup to the woman, couples will not be able to adapt to a future that will probably include the two-career marriage. The third option gives Liz and Paul the opportunity to stop asking the question "Who's most important?" The question they ask instead is "How can we both get the things we want from life and each other?" Since each considers the other's life important, they take turns supporting one another. One is satellite to the other upon request.

In an earlier chapter we mentioned that Paul has been the

Stefano's main money source for a number of years. Liz's psychology practice will soon bring an income equal to Paul's. In fact, the odds are good that her income will top his in a few years. They agree that when that happens, if Paul wishes he can quit his job. He can take time off to try a new career, go back to school, stay at home, or dabble in various interests.

In a traditional marriage a man has to be disabled, incompetent, or irresponsible in order to get time off from his role as provider. He may have a heart attack, a factory accident, manage to get himself fired from a position he has worked years to achieve, or run off with another woman. In a role-expanded marriage, the man gains an opportunity to share or possibly unload the endless responsibility as a breadwinner. The woman has an opportunity to share responsibility for maintaining their home and family.

The principle of sex-role expansion will become increasingly important in the future. An alternative marriage style must be created wherein the woman shares equal power in the relationship with her man. Older women/younger men couples have begun to make relationships that are models for equalizing power. A large number of these couples have been able to share earning, chores, and childrearing in unusual but satisfying ways.

We believe there are more older woman/younger man couples today because the relationship offers greater opportunity for role flexibility. Older women and younger men say they both benefit from expanding their sex roles. For instance, the woman is thrilled to have a man who is able to throw up a protective wall around her when she needs to direct her energies into work. It is the same wall that women have always built around men, the wall which fends off relatives, kids, salesmen, and broken appliances. The protective wall is one part of role expansion; supportive nurturance is another.

Older women love having a man who will plan and fix

meals, go shopping, and take over social planning. Young men are proud to be so accomplished, to be helpmates to their older wives. Younger men like being married to women who prefer to praise their accomplishments rather than nag constantly about what they aren't doing. Generally, the varying tasks of earning, domestic life, and child care flow back and forth between them as needed.

Role flexibility brings the freedom to open up choices rather than narrow them. It also brings disadvantages of an increased need for decision-making with a consequent need to take responsibility for decisions. Frequent adaptation and frequent decision-making creates greater anxiety.

In our time people want to be listened to, loved, and appreciated for what they have to offer. They want to be free to seek their goals in life and have a modicum of security. Role flexibility is one style of relationship, a third option, which can respond to our society's constant demand for change as well as the rising demand for personal fulfillment.

Older woman/younger man couples teach us to play down competition while playing up cooperation and mutual appreciation. They consciously lessen the power struggle. Rather than feel threatened by the woman's greater experience, money, or status, the younger men feel enhanced. For a variety of reasons they enjoy developing their sensitive, feminine side. Younger men do not expect older women to give up power; instead they agree to negotiate power.

The qualities that attract older women and younger men to one another are financial and emotional independence, role flexibility, the ability to discard inappropriate rules, and a willingness to share power. These qualities are the same ones that can create a solid, long-lasting relationship for a same-age couple in an ever-changing society.

NOTES

1. A CONTROVERSIAL RELATIONSHIP

1. Lisa Connolly, "Singleminded," *Westways*, April 1977, p. 12.
2. David Gelman, "How Men Are Changing," *Newsweek*, 16 January 1978, pp. 53-61.
3. Quoted in Gail Sheehy, *Passages*, p. 240.

2. WHO ARE THEY?

1. Theodora Kroeber-Quinn, "Cross Generation Marriage," *Co-Evolution Quarterly*, Fall 1976, p. 106.
2. Agatha Christie, *An Autobiography*, p. 500.

3. GOING PUBLIC

1. Kroeber-Quinn, "Cross Generation Marriage," p. 105.

4. PRIVATE FEARS

1. Los Angeles *Times*, 23 May 1978.

5. BREAKING RULES

1. Sigmund Freud, *The Basic Writings of Sigmund Freud*, ed. A. A. Brill, pp. 821-832.
2. *The New York Times*, "The Literary View," 15 January 1978, p. 29.
3. Anaïs Nin, *The Diary of Anaïs Nin, 1955–1966*, ed. Gunther Stuhlmann, p. 61.

6. POWER AND DOMINANCE

1. Los Angeles *Times*, 14 November 1978.
2. Jay Hailey, *Strategies of Psychotherapy*, pp. 10-11.
3. Herb Goldberg, *The Hazards of Being Male*, p. xi.
4. Gelman, "How Men Are Changing," *Newsweek*, p. 60.
5. Ibid.

7. WHO'S LOOKING FOR A MOTHER?

1. *National Enquirer*, 20 March 1979.
2. Ibid.
3. Nicholas Fraser, *Aristotle Onassis*, p. 54.
4. "At Long Last Love," *Newsweek*, 24 October 1977, p. 85.
5. Janet Chase-Marshall, "Who's Afraid of Phyllis Chesler?" *Human Behavior*, September 1978, p. 56.
6. Ibid.
7. "Older Women–Young Men," *Ebony*, May 1978, p. 78.
8. Phyllis Chesler, *About Men*, dedication.
9. *Human Behavior*, September 1978, p. 56.
10. Ibid.
11. Rollo May, *Power and Innocence*, p. 98.

8. MONEY AND STATUS

1. Ideas developed by Lynn Ramsey, *Gigolo*, pp. 73-82.

9. SEX

1. Goldberg, *Hazards of Being Male*, p. 23.
2. Quoted in Garson Kanin, *It Takes a Long Time to Become Young*, p. 63.
3. Gelman, "How Men Are Changing," *Newsweek*, 16 January 1978.

10. THE QUESTION OF CHILDREN

1. "Love Styles/Preview 79," *US*, 9 January 1979, p. 24.

11. THE SHARED EXPERIENCE

1. Quoted in Anthony West, *Mortal Wounds*, p. 220.
2. Sheldon Kopp, *If You Meet the Buddha on the Road, Kill Him*, p. 71.
3. Alvin Toffler, *Future Shock*, p. 228.

12. THE FUTURE IS NOW

1. Quoted in West, *Mortal Wounds*, p. 373.
2. Ralph G. Martin, *Jennie*, vol. 2, p. 181.
3. Ibid.

4. Ibid., p. 333.
5. Ibid., p. 355.
6. Ruth Gordon, *Myself among Others*, p. 224.
7. Kanin, *It Takes a Long Time to Become Young*, pp. 106-107.
8. Ibid., p. 110.

13. WHAT CAN WE LEARN?

1. Abraham H. Maslow, *Toward a Psychology of Being* (New York: D. Van Nostrand Company, 1968), p. 25.
2. Ibid., p. 25.
3. Ibid.
4. Ibid., p. 26.

BIBLIOGRAPHY

Andrews, Wayne, *Germaine: A Portrait of Madame de Staël*. New York: Atheneum, 1963.

Chesler, Phyllis. *About Men*. New York: Simon and Schuster, 1978.

Christie, Agatha. *An Autobiography*. New York: Ballantine Books, 1977.

"Delilah." *Older Woman, Younger Man: The New Look in Love*. New York: Pinnacle Books, 1975.

Fraser, Nicholas, Jacobson, Philip, Ottaway, Mark, and Chester, Lewis. *Aristotle Onassis*. New York: Ballantine Books, 1978.

Freud, Sigmund. *The Basic Writings of Sigmund Freud*. Edited by A. A. Brill. New York: Modern Library/Random House, 1938.

Gallant, Mavis, *The Affair of Gabrielle Russier*. New York: Knopf, 1971.

Goldberg, Herb. *The Hazards of Being Male*. New York: Signet/NAL, 1977.

Hailey, Jay. *Strategies of Psychotherapy*. New York: Grune and Stratton, 1963.

Herold, J. Christopher. *Mistress to an Age: A Life of Madame de Staël*. Indianapolis: Bobbs-Merrill, 1958.

Hutchinson, Roger, and Kahn, Gary. *A Family Affair: The Margaret and Tony Story*. New York: Two Continents/Bunch Books, 1977.

Justice, Blair, and Justice, Rita. *The Broken Taboo: Sex in the Family*. New York: Human Sciences Press, 1979.

Kanin, Garson. *It Takes a Long Time to Become Young*. New York: Doubleday & Co., Inc., 1978.

Kelen, Betty. *Mohammed: The Messenger of God*. Nashville: Nelson, 1975.

Kopp, Sheldon B. *If You Meet the Buddha on the Road, Kill Him!: The Pilgrimage of Psychotherapy Patients*. New York: Bantam Books, 1976.

Laing, R. D. *The Politics of the Family and Other Essays*. New York: Vintage Books (Random House), 1972.

Lucas, Robert. *Frieda Lawrence: The Story of Frieda von Richthofen and D. H. Lawrence*. New York: Viking, 1972.

MacShane, Frank. *The Life of Raymond Chandler*. New York: E. P. Dutton & Co., 1976.

Martin, Ralph G. *Jennie: The Life of Lady Randolph Churchill*, Volume 2. New York: Signet/NAL, 1972.

May, Rollo. *Power and Innocence: A Search for the Sources of Violence*. New York: Norton, 1972.

McCary, James Leslie. *Human Sexuality: A Brief Edition*. New York: D. Van Nostrand Co., 1973.

Mitchell, Yvonne. *Colette: A Taste for Life*. New York: Harcourt Brace Jovanovich, 1975.

Murdoch, Derrick. *The Agatha Christie Mystery*. London: Pagurian Press, 1976.

Nin, Anaïs. *The Diary of Anaïs Nin, 1955–1966*. Edited by Gunther Stuhlmann. New York: Harcourt Brace Jovanovich, 1976.

Radley, Virginia L. *Elizabeth Barrett Browning*. New York: Twayne, 1972.

Ramsey, Lynn. *Gigolos: The World's Best Kept Men*. Englewood Cliffs, N.J.: Prentice-Hall, Inc., 1978.

Sheehy, Gail. *Passages: Predictable Crises of Adult Life*. New York: E. P. Dutton & Co., Inc., 1976.

Toffler, Alvin. *Future Shock*. New York: Random House, 1970.

West, Anthony. *Mortal Wounds*. New York: McGraw-Hill, 1973.

Zilbergeld, Bernie. *Male Sexuality: A Guide to Sexual Fulfillment*. Boston: Little, Brown, 1978.

INDEX